Behavioral Economics

Behavioral Economics

Empowering Youth to Make Smart Choices

Jim Wasserman and Jiab Wasserman

ROWMAN & LITTLEFIELD
Lanham • Boulder • New York • London

Published by Rowman & Littlefield
An imprint of The Rowman & Littlefield Publishing Group, Inc.
4501 Forbes Boulevard, Suite 200, Lanham, Maryland 20706
www.rowman.com

86-90 Paul Street, London EC2A 4NE

Copyright © 2024 by James Wasserman and Jiab Wasserman

All rights reserved. No part of this book may be reproduced in any form or by any electronic or mechanical means, including information storage and retrieval systems, without written permission from the publisher, except by a reviewer who may quote passages in a review.

British Library Cataloguing in Publication Information Available

Library of Congress Cataloging-in-Publication Data

Names: Wasserman, Jim, 1961- author. | Wasserman, Jiab, author.
Title: Behavioral economics : empowering youth to make smart choices / Jim Wasserman, Jiab Wasserman.
Description: Lanham : Rowman & Littlefield, 2023. | Includes bibliographical references. | Summary: "To help empower children to be resilient and have more self-guidance in their own development, this book explores the general process of how we make choices, from consciously rational to subconsciously emotional. Through exploratory lessons supplied in each chapter, kids learn the techniques of effective choice-making so that they have the tools to stand against outside sways. Special attention is given to instill in youth tools for positive and effective choices in both worlds they live in, "real life" and online"—Provided by publisher.
Identifiers: LCCN 2023028337 (print) | LCCN 2023028338 (ebook) | ISBN 9781475872552 (cloth) | ISBN 9781475872569 (paperback) | ISBN 9781475872576 (ebook)
Subjects: LCSH: Economics—Study and and teaching (Middle school)—United States. | Choice (Psychology)—Study and and teaching (Middle school)—United States. | Economics—Psychological aspects | Youth—Psychology. | Youth—United States—Social conditions.
Classification: LCC LB1584.75 .W37 2023 (print) | LCC LB1584.75 (ebook) | DDC 155.4/1383—dc23/eng/20230913
LC record available at https://lccn.loc.gov/2023028337
LC ebook record available at https://lccn.loc.gov/2023028338

Contents

Acknowledgements	vii
Preface: Taking on the Wizards behind the Curtain	ix
Introduction	xi
1 Meet the Chooser (That Would Be *You*)	1
2 How Do We Make Choices?	7
3 Nonrational Factors in Choosing	23
4 Nudges, or External Factors on Our Choices	37
5 Sway	57
6 The Tween Mind	87
7 Millennial, Gen Z, and Gen A Life	123
Glossary	155
Bibliography	163
About the Authors	167

Acknowledgements

This book series is about what influences people's choices and actions. True to the books' premises, there were many people who influenced and guided us over the past year and a half we wish to acknowledge.

We are grateful to everyone at Rowman & Littlefield who helped make the series come to print. At the top of that group is Tom Koerner. Tom guided us from the initial concept to the material formation of the book as it now stands. Likewise, Jasmine Holman was instrumental in being our "this is your next step" guide in the process, keeping us going in the right direction. Michael Hals was our nuts & bolts editor who rounded out the team.

Closer to home, we cannot adequately express our appreciation to all our friends, who no doubt regretted the time commitment invoked by their casual question, "What have you been up to?" Two special people deserve note. Kennedy Zapata-Schleicher was our guide to, "What do younger people think about this?" as well as a supportive interpreter of social media. David Loveland was the fellow teacher and friend who gave us council with the perfect combination of constructive sagacity and snark, the hallmark of a master educator.

Of course, we could have done none of this without the love and support of our closest family members. Besides these three cats, however, we also love and appreciate our sons, Ben & Journey, for their encouragement, patience, and guidance. It's rewarding for parents to see their children no longer need them. Don't misunderstand; you two still need us, but we are grateful for the developing self-sufficiency that gave us time to write.

Finally, we want to thank our parents, Noa, Doris, Suebpong and Komkai. You lived as couples on either side of the world. In many ways your lives couldn't have been more different. Still, you shared the common trait of having been wonderful, supportive parents. In a world that seems nowadays where everyone seeks to be styled as "influencers," we couldn't have asked for better influencers and role models for ourselves than you four. If readers find good guidance for youth in our words, they should know you four are speaking through us. We dedicate this book series to you.

Preface

Taking on the Wizards behind the Curtain

If you or the young people you intend to instruct with the material in this book have not seen the movie *The Wizard of Oz*,[1] we highly recommend you stop and do so before we proceed with this intro. Go ahead; we'll wait.

The "great and powerful" wizard of Oz appears as a giant, green, ghostly head amid fire and noise, telling Dorothy and her friends they must do as he says. It's only when Toto the dog eventually pulls back the curtain that they see the "wizard" is just an ordinary man pulling levers, trying to trick them into doing his bidding.

Consider us Totos. We are determined to pull back the curtain, revealing the wizards who pull levers to sway and nudge kids with their messaging. The wizards use their devices and artifices to awe youth into disregarding their own sense of identity and sensibilities to be the pliable subjects the wizards wish them to be.

Unlike Dorothy, today's real-life wizards don't need a tornado or a bump to the head to whisk them to Oz. The great and powerful show wizards influence youth through the power of ubiquitous media.

Just as Dorothy saw Kansas and Oz as distinct but overlapping, we also need to consider the two worlds that young people grow up in and receive messaging. Older people tend to focus more IRL, or in real life.[2] It's important to realize, however, that for younger people, what transpires online can be just as real and impactful to them as what happens IRL.

We oldsters can remember hanging out principally with kids our own age from our own childhood through early teen years. We began independent socialization in age-limited, secluded sandboxes. Many youths today, however, are first exploring the world, making choices, and forming ideas based on those choices in adult-saturated circumstances. Most youth activities are heavily adult monitored. That may sound all good, but it also limits the space youth have to explore, choose, and learn for themselves. As for their online world, it's adult filled but unmonitored, at least by adults looking out for the youth. It's one big sandbox containing people of all ages and points of view, with good and bad intentions. Youth may not even know that the other "kid" they are chatting with is a very adult person with their own purpose.

When youth are eager to start their exploration of their worlds in search of hidden treasure, many educators focus on teaching kids how to search and dig for it. Our focus here includes that, but we also want to take a step back. Before the kids start digging where they are told "X marks the spot," we want to start a conversation with them about what they consider to be treasure worth digging for. Kids today are caught in a tornado of voices telling them what is worthy of their desire and effort from media to the celebrity everyone wants to imitate to the new unknown "friend" online. Youth need the skills and self-awareness to determine what's of value for themselves.

In *The Wizard of Oz,* Dorothy's companions—and even Dorothy herself—don't get what they are seeking from the wizard. He merely gives them tokens that symbolically recognize what they already have had and used. The Scarecrow receives a diploma celebrating the brain that he has been using all along. The Tin Man gets a heart-watch testimonial to signify the compassion he has shown. The Cowardly Lion receives a medal for previously used courage. Dorothy realizes she has had the power to go where she wanted to all along, by clicking her heels in the shoes.

So let's teach kids about the powers they can develop for themselves as they travel roads, yellow brick, virtual, or otherwise. They don't need outside wizards to confront witches. They just need their own powers, some faithful friends, and maybe a smart dog.

NOTES

1. Normally, we recommend the book over any movie version, but the visuals in the movie are important here.
2. Hereafter we will often use the popular online abbreviation "IRL" as denoting something occurring physically, beyond the online world.

Introduction

One of the signs of the back-to-school season for teachers is a compulsary in-service program. Sometimes going by "professional enrichment" or some other catchy name, they most often involve an expert brought in from outside the school who makes a presentation on some facet of education or child development theory. Unfortunately, the experts sometimes have limited actual in-classroom experience, reminding veterans of a war strategist who has never actually seen a battlefield. There are some common elements to such presentations, such as being a long lecture on why lecturing is a terrible modality for communicating, with breakout sessions afterwards that involve varying degrees of teachers discussing the material and catching up from summer break.

Given this common experience of teachers, allow us, before we tell you what we are doing in this book, to say there are two things we do NOT do here.

We do not dwell in purely theoretical terms. Teachers, of course, know their stuff. That doesn't mean, however, they want the material they use to be presented to them in high academic terms. In reviewing a lesson we once designed, a fellow academic asked, "What does this lesson do for semiotics?" We knew what *semiotics* meant but asked the academic how they thought that term applied to practical, in-the-classroom teaching of middle schoolers. "I don't know," was the reply. "I am just asking questions."

High language may be correct, but it is not proper if it doesn't serve to promote the topic when it needs to. Teachers are multitasking with multiple students from the moment the class starts. They need and want the equivalent of an effective plug-and-play accessory rather than the intricate components of raw theory that they are then expected to assemble and modify in their spare time into working devices modulated for each student. In every concept we present here, we strive to put it in easy-to-communicate terms so that teachers—and, for that matter, parents, counselors, and even kids themselves—can grasp the concept and run with it. Surely, there are more academic, esoteric explorations of media literacy, but they are not tailored for immediate use with young minds just transitioning to include abstract thought.

We do not lay out an entire, new course of study. Speaking of including semiotics—or not—every teacher has been asked why they do not include something extra in their curriculum, such as other novels, another part of history or geography, personal finance, or a deep dive into an emerging science. They are all good ideas, but the suggestions fade when the teacher politely responds, "That's a great idea. What do I take *out* of the curriculum to make room?"

Every teacher is an economist. They are experts at efficient use of the scarcest resource: time. As such, any suggestion to include more topics or material, including media literacy, are met with consternation. So we have designed lessons in this book that cover media literacy while also overlapping as much as possible with already-established subjects, such as literature and math. Social science methodology is included to pair it with physical sciences. The lessons can thus serve a dual purpose rather than being a diversion from what often is required by state mandates.

To make the lessons integratable, we have had to choose some areas of media literacy to omit. As we will discuss later, the term *media literacy* is still being defined. Some see it as including the skills to make a podcast. Others see it as including a full study of communication. Would that it all could be taught, but it can't.

We focus on something universal to all aspects of the wide field: the skills of choice making that are the heart of behavioral economics. That in itself is a big topic. So we have divided the education of children in choice making into two books. This book explores the skills for choosing in general. Developmental psychology and behavioral economics help show how the process of autonomous choosing develops in young people. We address the choice-selection process of young people broadly, with occasional specific focus on online decision-making. You can find further exploration of the particulars of online choices, including the outside influences on those choices, in our companion book to this.[1]

We have tried not to make this book a list of "thou shalt / shalt nots" for you to pass on to youth. That is an ineffective and poorly received way to instruct. Rather, our approach is to outline principles and concepts that young people can then apply in their daily lives. In many ways it is like teaching about good nutrition. Just as it is impossible to designate all foods as consumable or not consumable, it is better to teach principles of healthy consumption and leave it to young people to apply those principles in their choices of food and ingredients. We believe the same approach works for consuming messaging and the ideas embedded in it.

You will find that each chapter, as it examines a topic, also provides *exploratories* for youth to see how the concepts covered play out in the real world. We don't want students to just think about what we tell them about messaging but to think about what *they* experience. How is it the same or different from the way we describe it? How does it vary by circumstance? Most importantly, *why* is it the same or different?

The exploratories in this book are, for several reasons, not designed to be airtight clinical investigations free of confounding variables. Aside from allowing us to avoid having to devote chapters to regression analysis and other concepts of statistics and advanced math, our goal is to give students who are first examining media a simple, visceral experience. We do ask at times for kids to reflect on methodology. Simultaneously, however, we want them to have fun, to have a freedom to wander and wonder that will carry the learning forward.

Educators should also feel free to modify the explorations as best fits your young explorers. We provide several follow-up questions covering what we hope is a wide variety of topics and ideas for a spectrum of ages. True to our word, it's your choice! For advanced students, feel free to encourage some extra, thoughtful thinking afterward, such as, "What might be changed that would get a different result?" If an exploration goes wrong, ask why it did so and what could be done better next time. The skill of reflection isn't just for social scientists but for anyone trying to successfully navigate life and ultimately make their own choices.

There is one last thing. We have designed the book principally for teachers. However, anyone who wants to promote media literacy and behavioral economics skills in students will find the topics and lessons in the book accessible and fun to do with youth—counselors, parents looking to supplement their child's education, and anyone else looking to better prepare the next generation for media and messaging we can't even imagine today. Because it's not about what the messengers do or how they do it; it's about what the kids are prepared to handle.

NOTE

1. *The Social Media Diet: A Guide for Young People to Be Smart Online Users and Consumers* is available on finer internet sites near you.

Chapter One

Meet the Chooser (That Would Be *You*)

A truism of life is that, once you unpack something, it's nearly impossible to get it all back into the container it came in. The same is true for knowledge. Learning is messy. It takes something everyone knows, like "Everything falls down," and blows it up into messy subparts with complications. Why do things fall? What does "down" mean? Does everything fall the same way, at the same rate? It's frustrating when you want a simple answer or rule of thumb to go by, but it's the cost of understanding.

The same is true for studying human behavior, only more so. If two rocks fell twenty thousand years ago because of an earthquake, the laws of physics can be used to understand what happened. If the rocks fell because two cave people each threw one, we would now have a whole bunch of extra questions. Was one accidental because he lost his grip, while the other was on purpose because she thought, "Why am I wasting my time holding a rock instead of painting a cave?" Maybe one didn't want to be seen with a rock, because it wasn't as cool as a handmade ax. How much thought did each person even put into the whole situation? Or was it just an impulsive moment? And maybe we should be more concerned with the saber-toothed cat that charged at them after being irritated by their throwing rocks?

The act of making a choice seems a simple thing. It's most always premised on the thought beginning with "I want." But social sciences have opened up that package as well and, like everything else, have released a lot of inner-working parts that seem more complicated and bigger than the package containing them. Why do I want option A over option B? Would I always choose option A over option B? What could make me change my mind? And how much of my choice is really mine?

Later than our cave people but still over twenty-five hundred years ago, people in ancient Greece came to the Temple of Apollo in Delphi to ask the gods questions. They would receive answers by way of prophecies delivered by priestesses. As people approached the temple, they passed through an open porch with columns. On the columns were written maxims, or short statements, supposedly said by the god Apollo to guide people as they sought knowledge. The first and most famous that people saw was *Gnōthi seauton* (Know yourself). In other words, before you check out the world, let alone try to peek into the future, you have to know who you are and what you bring as you try to understand things.

Today that maxim still applies, from trying to understand the physical world to the online one. When you start a role-playing game, what's the first thing you usually do? You check out your attributes and skills; maybe you even designate where you want your strengths and skills to be. People choose a class or type of player, apply skill points, and maybe even put on skins,[1] all making each player a different combination of attributes as they set to accomplish things in the game world. The final touch is the gamer's personalized style of play.

So let's begin to unpack the process of how we make choices. We first need to know ourselves and how we operate. We need to know our skills and strengths, as well as how we approach choice making. We also should get a quick idea of what factors, internal and external, affect our choice making. Then, like the people visiting the Temple of Apollo, we can get inside to the deeper stuff.

NOTE

1. Skins are changes to the outer appearance of a player's avatar. They normally don't change the artificial intelligence (AI) gameplay, though in cooperative gaming, they can affect what other players think and how they react to the player.

Chapter 1 Accompanying Lessons

LESSON 1.1. GETTING TO KNOW YOU

Focus of Exploration

Understanding how preferences and personality develop over time.

Intro Questions / Thoughts for Students

We tend to describe ourselves in the present with "I am" or "I like," but how long has this "you" been you? Did all the things that you are now develop at once? Or did they evolve slowly over time?

Activity

Fill out table 1.1 below:

Table 1.1. Getting to Know My Choosy Self

	My Favorite ...	My Earliest Memory of Trying It	A Standout Memory I Have about It	A Person Who Helped Me to Like It	Other Reasons It Became My Favorite
Food					
Color					
Animal					
Subject in school					
Activity in my free time					

If you need help remembering, talk with a parent or someone who has known you for a long time.

Follow-Up Questions/Discussions

Were there any categories where you couldn't decide on one favorite thing or where your favorite changed a lot? Why do you think that one category changed a lot but another did not?

Part of studying people, including yourself, is looking for patterns. Do you see any patterns or things in common among your answers? Maybe it was at about the same age that you found things to be your favorite? Maybe you picked up a lot of favorites from an older brother or sister or a best friend?

We focused here on what we like, but can you do the same with what you dislike? Is who you are defined as much by what you don't like as what you do like? How so or not?

Choosing often seems like a simple "I want this now" decision. If you are choosing a food that has been a favorite going back a while, however, it's like all the versions of you going back in the past are also voting for that food. How does that affect your thinking that you might try something different?

There is an old thought experiment called the ship of Theseus. Imagine a very old wooden ship that was owned by the legendary Greek hero Theseus some 2,500 years ago. We still have the ship, but over time, some of the boards rot or break so slowly that the boards are replaced one by one over the years until, now, every part of the ship was added after Theseus. Is it still Theseus' ship? If not, when did it stop being *his* ship? How does this thought experiment relate to you changing your favorite things? When you change what is your favorite or make another choice, are you still you? Are you a "new you?"

LESSON 1.2. LET'S GET THIS PARTY STARTED!

Focus of Exploration

Understanding yourself and others as individual choosers.

Intro Questions / Thoughts for Students

When you are working in a group, what would you say are the skills, talents, and knowledge that you bring to help the group be successful? What skills, talents, and knowledge do you often rely on others to have to help you when working in a group?

Do your skills that you contribute to a group change with different groups, such as being with family versus being with friends? What about the same group, such as with friends, but in different situations?

Activity

Imagine your family or your friends are forming a party around going on an adventure, like in a movie or game. It can be real, like a big family vacation, or fantasy, such as you and your friends on a monster quest. Acting as a character in the adventure, rate everyone in your party as you assess them in real life on a one-to-five (low-to-high) scale for the following:

- Physical strength/toughness
- Problem solving and other mental challenges
- Determination: (stamina, staying, and focus power)
- Dexterity: quickness in reaction or ability to change and adapt to new circumstances
- Personality: likeability, getting along/cooperating with others, persuasion of others, resolving conflicts

Also list any special skills you and each member of your party has in real life, such as sneakiness or ability to fix broken things.

Follow-Up Questions/Discussions

Does your party have a good balance of skills? What skills are your party weak in? Who might you add that could help?

What other skills besides the ones listed are important or need their own category? Are there special skills needed for a particular outing or mission?

When is it better to preplan how the group will address a challenge, and when is it better to take things as they come and let everyone do what they can? What are the advantages to each style? Who goes by each style in your party?

For a party you are a part of IRL, how are leadership and/or final choices determined? Does one person make the final call? Is there a vote? Do you like the system? How might you change or suggest changing the choice-selection process?

If you could add three extra points to your skills, where would you add them? What about adding one special ability? How could you add points like that or the special skill to yourself in real life? Would it be reading more, working out more, or doing something less?

Chapter Two

How Do We Make Choices?

One of the first words a child learns to use is "No!" It's usually mastered by toddlers at around eighteen months. It's perfected by teens sometime before eighteen years.

Understanding and asserting "No!" seems like a negative event, but it's actually an important first step to a person's independence. The toddler is making *a choice,* and having a choice may be one of the most powerful abilities in the world. Being able to say "Will I take option A or option B?" defines being a conscious entity. It is the essence of power,[1] even privilege.[2] (See lesson 2.1.)

It feels good, even powerful, to have a choice. A quick internet search for advertising that includes "choice," "choose," or similar words shows how often marketers acknowledge a consumer's choice and use that to make the consumer feel they are in control.[3] They express appreciation that the consumer has used his or her power to consider the marketer's product or message. They have gratitude that the consumer's independent choice-making journey led them to the marketer's door or website. Are the marketers genuine? We'll get to that. (See lesson 2.2.)

Choice is so important to us that there is an entire *social science* devoted to it: *economics*. "Wait!" we hear you say. "I thought economics was about money?" The answer is "Kinda."[4]

When we are choosing between option A or option B, we do so because we don't have the *resources* to have both. A woodworker might have just enough lumber to make a bench or a table but not enough to make both. Which should he make? That's an economic choice.

For most choices the two most commonly demanded resources are money and time. No one has an unlimited amount of either, so we spend our lives choosing how best to use these two *scarce* resources. Since money is usually the more immediate and tangible of the two resources, economists have given most of their attention to money, especially around their paycheck time. (See lesson 2.3.)

For students time is often the scarce resource. They need to do homework but also want to chat with friends; maybe watch a funny, short video; or even watch a movie. If students had unlimited time, they could do it all, but (like everyone else) they don't. So they have to learn how to make choices.

Because time is a scarce resource, the people who want your time or attention design systems to grab and hold your attention as long as they can. The internet, for example, is designed to keep you glued to it. Companies make money by how often and how long people keep their eyeballs on their content and ads. They will put a catchy *eye-candy* graphic or a *clickbait* headline to pause your scrolling and site hopping. You then make a general, unbounded choice, called a *metadecision*, to check it out. Once on a site, you'll find there are few clocks or other reminders of time, so you forget about how you are spending that scarce resource.[5] There are often no page numbers on sites—just long, endless scrolls—so you keep scrolling without a mental break to remind you how far down the page you are or how much time you have spent. The open-endedness combined with the possibility that the next post might be interesting keep you going. It is exactly what the site or app designer wants you to do, even as they say it is your choice. (See lesson 2.4.)

The key to good, rational choice making is called a *cost-benefit analysis*. Let's say a student is choosing between watching videos or getting a school project done. By a cost-benefit analysis, the student would first compare the benefits of watching the movie (fun!) with the benefits of getting the project done (good grade). If the student could quantify those benefits, like how important those benefits are to her on a scale of one to ten,[6] it would help to make the choice more concrete.

A problem in cost-benefit analysis is that many people stop after comparing only benefits. A true cost-benefit analysis would also consider the cost of choosing the movie—the student feels guilty for letting her project group down—and the cost of choosing to do the project—she can't join the fun chat with friends to talk about the movie the next day. Sometimes, the costs can outweigh the benefits.[7] (See lesson 2.5.)

Another problem humans have in making rational choices is how hard it is to think about the future and the impact of our choices down the road. What if the same student from before chooses to both watch the movie and do the project? She then stays up late—very late. She is able to do both, but the next day, she is beat. She has the info for the project but is so tired she forgets what she has to say. She chats with friends about the movie but has trouble following along with all the conversation threads. By the end of the day, she is so sluggish she doesn't play well in the big game.

We can also have problems with *delayed gratification*. We want to enjoy things now, even if the enjoyment of the alternative might be greater later.[8] At the moment of choice, many will ask themselves, "Who knows if things will work out? We can't know the future for sure, so why take the gamble?" We also prefer the certainty of gratification now even when risking having to pay a great cost later. Many middle schoolers can't resist the temptation to say or do something that will get instant laughs from their friends even at the risk of being sent to the principal or facing other discipline. The reward of being funny and the center of attention in the moment is too great to resist.[9] (See lesson 2.6.)

Speaking of later, I've found every person carries in their mind an imaginary superhero who will fix any future problem arising from the present choice. That superhero can be called *Future-Me*.[10] Future-Me will not be tired no matter how hard or how much you strain now. Future-Me will be able to finish the project at lunch so I can goof off now. Future-Me will be able to fake having done what I told people I did so I can now choose to do something else.

People sometimes shrug off bad things as somebody else's problem. Eating lunch, someone lets wrappers fall on the ground. Pointing out the trash, he might shrug as he walks away, saying, "Somebody else will clean it up." Of course this is wrong to do to someone else, and chances are that the mess will get grosser. Inconsiderate as this is, though, people are doing the same thing when they leave problems to Future-Me, and what's really weird is that the person they are inconveniencing and not caring about is still them! (See lesson 2.7.)

If we struggle IRL to remember that choices today have consequences tomorrow, the internet is even more intensive on focusing on choices *now* while ignoring potential consequences later.[11] The internet has little regard for what Future-Me might have to clean up—or live with. Ask students to think of a joke or a comment they made, a dare they took, or a stunt they pulled when they were younger and that they now regret.[12] It may have been funny at the moment, so they chose to do it. They didn't think and just acted. Now ask the students to imagine if a video of them doing that embarrassing thing had been around for new friends who didn't know them back then to see it.[13] Imagine that every time they start a new school or join a new group, that video is played or at least offered for people to watch.[14] There are a lot of Future-Mes right now doing a lot of unhappy cleanup work of what their Previous-Me did in the past.

NOTES

1. "Where there is no decision there is no life."—JJ Dewey
2. Unfortunately for many, having a choice is beyond their power or circumstances. As Oprah Winfrey has said, "Understand that the right to choose your own path is a sacred privilege."
3. See chapter 7 regarding the idea of consumer sovereignty.
4. Social scientists, dealing with inconsistent and irrational chunks of human behavior, are much more comfortable with the concept of "kinda" than physical scientists.
5. Casinos also have few clocks and few windows to help people forget about time passing. Children and parents can attest to the different conceptual boundaries of time regarding the phrase "Sit for a minute."
6. If you want to be economist fancy, call them units of *utility*.
7. There is a lot more to cost-benefit analysis, but we made the choice to save room here. If you are interested in more about how young people can make better choices with systems like cost-benefit analysis, you might choose to check out chapter 2 of our 2019 book *Middle Schoolers, Meet Media Literacy*.
8. See the famous marshmallow challenge: James Clear, "The Marshmallow Experiment and the Power of Delayed Gratification," published January 23, 2014, https://jamesclear.com/delayed-gratification. Try it!
9. One of the authors here still falls prey to this be-funny-now temptation, fifty years beyond middle school.
10. Jim Wasserman, "Saving the Day," *HumbleDollar*, February 12, 2022, https://humbledollar.com/2022/02/saving-the-day/.
11. Of course, there is no single entity called *the internet*. What we call the internet is the collective experience or system that has evolved, in much the same way people refer to life.
12. They don't have to say it out loud (to avoid embarrassment), but incidents involving bathrooms and related activities are common here. So are sports and other performance mess-ups.
13. Even if it wasn't recorded, parents will hold on to the embarrassing memory for the child and are more than happy to retell it at family gatherings or when friends are over at the house or recount it in graphic detail to the person their child is dating one day.
14. Two of the biggest misleading promises of the internet are that something can be *deleted* and that something can be made *private*. Nothing is private online, and nothing is truly deleted.

Chapter 2 Accompanying Lessons

LESSON 2.1. HOW MANY FORKS DO YOU SEE?

Focus of Exploration

Presence of so many choices in life.

Intro Questions / Thoughts for Students

You hear about forks in the road. Sometimes, people say they approach a crossroads. What do these phrases mean? Can you think of stories where the protagonist came to a fork or a crossroads either literally or figuratively?

We use words like power or privilege a lot, but what do they mean? What do they look like?

How does having a choice relate to having power or privilege?

Activity

First, make an estimate of how many choices, or forks in the road, you will have in the next thirty minutes. Will it be more or less than ten? Twenty-five? Fifty?

Then using a tally sheet, try to record as many of the choices you make. For each fork in the road, identify where each path led, which path you chose, and whether it was an easy, medium, or hard choice to make.

You have limited choices when being between two options, a fork, but you will often have more options than that, a crossroads. Don't worry. It's the number of choices we are looking for, not the number of options for each choice.

You will have to pay close attention to find them. Did someone call out to you, and you responded? That was a choice. If you are hungry and get something to eat, not only is which food you ate a choice, but the first decision to go get food was a choice! And don't forget the routes you take to get someplace!

This also may work better if you have a friend who points out choices you may miss, and then you switch turns.

Follow-Up Questions/Discussions

Is it difficult to get all the choices? Even simple things like whether to do or not do something counts as a choice as long as both options are available to you.

Is how you treat others a choice as well?

Go back to your definition of power or privilege. Many people describe those as having desirable things like money. What if you had lots of money but no choice on how to spend it? Would you still call that power and privilege? Which do you think is more important, having wealth or choices?

Are there areas where you wish you had more choice? What are those areas? Why? What can you do to give yourself more choice in that area? Can one choice lead to more choices in the area you want?

Some people like to say "I had no choice" when what they are saying is they did not like one of the options. Do you think that is the same thing?

Are there some parts of your life where you are glad you don't have a choice? What are those areas? Why are you glad?

LESSON 2.2. THANK YOU FOR CHOOSING US

Focus of Exploration

Use of "choice" in messaging.

Intro Questions / Thoughts for Students

Have you ever been thanked for making a choice, and it surprised you? Maybe you didn't consciously make the choice, or you really had no choice but to do what they were thanking you for? Maybe you had to buy something like school supplies, but the store thanked you for your choice?

Activity

Look for ads or promotions that use the word "choice," "choose," or some variation of that. They might also use synonyms like "options" or "possibilities."

Follow-Up Questions/Discussions

Social scientists look at the messy noise of messaging and human interaction and look for patterns that might tell them something. For example, they ask if are there any particular products or services that seem to talk about choice more than others? Was there a difference between ads for things people need to buy (necessities) and things people like to buy (luxuries)?

How is the word "choice" used? Is it just a statement like "You have a choice"? Or is it part of a thank-you for choosing them? Do the different ways choice is discussed make you feel different?

Were there any ads that mentioned or thanked you for your choice, but you felt you really didn't have much choice about it? How did you feel?

A rule of advertising is that the viewer of the ad should feel good after hearing about the product. How does talking about choice in the ad do this? Do you feel appreciated or empowered? Is that the goal of the ad? Do you think that having positive feelings while looking at an ad for a brand makes you like that brand more, even just a little bit?

Do you think sellers who have a lot of competition thank buyers more or less than or equal to those who don't have competition? How do you feel when someone chooses you, such as to be on a team, when you know they have a choice?

After looking at how ads use the word "choice" and their thanking you, reflect on how you appreciate or express thanks for when people choose you. Do you thank them enough? Too much? When is it appropriate?

LESSON 2.3. TIME OR MONEY?

Focus of Exploration

Scarce resources, including time and money. How to conduct a survey.

Intro Questions / Thoughts for Students

When you hear people of different ages, such as kids your age, teens, young adults, and older adults, talk about not having enough of something, do you hear common statements within the age-groups? Do you hear common or different statements between the age-groups?

Activity

This is a survey where you will be interviewing people and recording their responses. It is recommended that you ask the questions in the same way of each person. Also, if they ask questions, try not to answer, but just ask them to respond as best they can. Be sure to ask the questions in the same order:

1. How old are you?
2. What is something that you wish you had more of?
3. If you had a choice between having more money, time, or something else, what would it be? You can only choose one.
4. What is something that you are grateful for having plenty of?

After you have interviewed at least ten people of different ages, try to make a graph of their responses to the question 3. Put the age of respondents on the x-axis. The y-axis can represent the number of responses saying money, time, or something else, using three different colors so you can see them side by side. You can alternatively make a pie chart.

Follow-Up Questions/Discussions

Do you see any patterns? Is one age-group wanting more time, or another, more money? Something else? What can you conclude about what is most desired but not available—scarcest—to people at different ages? Draw lines on the x-axis to mark off the preteens, teens, and adults both under and over forty (or any other way you wish). Are there any patterns?

If there is no clear pattern, that does not mean the investigation was a waste. That may prove that age is *not* a factor in what people want. Maybe other things in life make them miss money or time more, like whether they have children. Also, might interviewing more people or a bigger variety of people give different results?

There is a reason for the order of questions. Question 1 is easiest and gets people who answer (*respondents*) into a question-answering mood. Question 2 is to get them to give their gut response. If you started with question 3, people might take your mentioning money or time as the focus of their choice rather than what they would have first said, like friendship.

Did the respondent's expression change when you shifted to asking about good things? Does that tell you anything about how our mood can be changed by what we are asked to think about?

Surveys are good to get a quick snapshot of how a person feels. Another way is by interviewing people to get more depth. For example, after the survey, ask people if their response would have been different at different times in their life or just on a different day. Most of all, let them talk and listen. You can learn a lot this way!

LESSON 2.4. SPEND SOME TIME WITH US

Focus of Exploration

Metadecision and spending of time online.

Intro Questions / Thoughts for Students

Do you think you are good about spending time wisely? How about guessing how much time has gone by?

Activity

Spend thirty minutes on the web. Don't set the alarm, but stop when *you* think it has been thirty minutes. Cover up any clocks, such as minimizing the taskbar if it has the time on it. (It's best not to do this with an app on a phone, as it is difficult not to see the time). As a bonus, use a web tracker that keeps tabs on where you go and how much time you were there. Google has an extension, and there are others that track time.

Follow-Up Questions/Discussions

You were doing this while intentionally trying to be conscious of time. Would there be a difference if you weren't doing this as an exploration but more casually, like when you really choose to just spend "a couple of minutes" online?

For the sites you visited, how many showed you real time passing? Why do many sites and games not show you the time?

Do you think more people underspend (less than thirty minutes) or overspend (more than thirty minutes)? Why do you think that is? Do you think it is the same as spending money, another scarce resource? Have you ever bought something because it is "only a couple of dollars" and then another and another till you end up having a lot less money?

Have you ever been trapped by the "just a little bit more time" mentality, and then you end up spending a lot more than you wanted to? Why do a lot of people do this? How can you prevent this?

If you used a web tracker, did you go to any new sites *after* the thirty minutes were already up rather than just running over time on a site? What is the difference?

Part of the difficulty of keeping an awareness of time is that you have to dedicate part of your mind to not being in the fun activity but being the monitor, which is not a lot of fun. What can you do to help the monitor part of your mind, such as using alarms and other tools?

LESSON 2.5. THE BENEFITS OF CONSIDERING COSTS

Focus of Exploration

How to do a *cost-benefit analysis*.

Intro Questions / Thoughts for Students

When you must choose between two options, like studying or having fun online, how do you decide? Do you go with your gut feeling, or do you think about the good and bad of each?

Activity

Choose something where you have two options that both have benefits. It can be something you have to choose now or you know will be a choice later, such as studying or playing a game. Use table 2.1. An example calculation is provided.

Table 2.1. Cost-Benefit Calculation

Choices	Good Things You Like from Doing This Option	From 1 (Low) to 10 (High), How Much Do You Like Those Good Things? "G-Value"	Bad Things You Don't Like but Will Happen from Doing This Option	From 1 (Low) to 10 (High), How Much Do You Not Like Those Bad Things? "B-Value"	For Each Option, Subtract the Value of the Bad from the Value of the Good (G–B)
Option A:					
Option B:					
Example Option A: Watch a movie	Fun	9	May not do well or fail the test	8	1
Example Option B: Study for a big test	Good grade	7	Not much fun	5	2

The number in the last column is the cost-benefit score of each option.

Here you should do option B, studying, because even though watching a movie has a higher short-term benefit (a value of 9), the cost of doing badly in school later makes its total less (only 1).

Follow-Up Questions/Discussions

Does the option with the higher final cost-benefit score match the option your gut told you to choose? If not, why do you think there is a difference?

Two people can think about the same choices and assign different values. That's because how much they like a benefit or don't like a cost is different for each person. Have someone else try the same choices you thought about, and see if their numbers match yours.

Even the same person can have different numbers for the same choices but at different times. A cost may seem bad at one time or not so bad at another. Have you had a time where you had the same choices as before but you changed your mind about which option you chose?

Often, we can come up with a compromise where we don't have to make it just one or the other. We can split time to do homework and then spend any time left over having fun. Other times, we must choose. What are examples of each for you?

Doing a cost-benefit analysis like this can help, but it does take time. What kind of choices do not need this detailed thinking out, and what kind of choices might benefit from you taking some time to do this kind of thinking through, even before the choice comes up?

LESSON 2.6. WAITER, WHAT'S THIS FLY DOING IN MY SOUP?

Focus of Exploration

Delayed gratification.

Intro Questions / Thoughts for Students

When you know something good can happen in the future, but you have to wait for it, how good are you at waiting? Are you patient? Do you worry that something will prevent the good thing from happening? Do your parents or friends agree with your self-assessment?

When are you willing to wait and risk not getting something to possibly get something better later? When are you willing to take a lesser but sure thing now?

Activity

Try to think back on two events:

- What is something you waited to get (not taking a shortcut or taking less sooner) that you are glad you waited for?
- When was a time you waited to get a thing, but something went wrong and you regret not taking the lesser but sure good thing sooner?

Be sure to include whether, looking back, you made the right choice.

Based on these two (or more) events, try to form a rule about whether you should wait for good things. When is it better to wait for a greater reward? When is it better to take a sure, lesser thing now? Does it matter how long you have to wait or how good the good thing will be?

Now, try to live by this rule for a few days or even a week, and see what happens.

Follow-Up Questions/Discussions

Did you change the rule to improve it? Did you ever end up with an always workable rule? Why or why not?

A quick experiment you can also do is to think of your favorite snack, such as a cookie. Try a rule in which every time you want one, you can have just one or have to wait thirty minutes. After that time, roll a die: a one equals no cookie at all; two to a four, one cookie; and five to six, two cookies! Will you take the one or wait?

Do other people have the same risk-taking desire or reluctance as you do for delayed gratification? Why do people differ?

Waiting is hard, so how can you help yourself wait for a bigger reward later? Some people put a picture of what they want so they can see it and be reminded not to spend now, such as when saving money for a trip or to buy something. What things like that can you do to help you wait and get a bigger reward? Another trick is to find immediate substitutes that can fill in just a bit until the waiting is over. You struggle to wait to see a friend, but you can send a quick text message till then. What are the advantages and potential problems of this technique?

There is a famous story about rewards over time involving rice and a chessboard. Read it and think about what the moral is. Here is one version: https://purposefocuscommitment. medium.com/the-rice-and-the-chess-board-story-the-power-of-exponential-growth-b1f7bd70aaca.

How Do We Make Choices?

LESSON 2.7. ROOM 222

Focus of Exploration

Thinking about choices in different time perspectives.

Intro Questions / Thoughts for Students

Have you ever made a choice that felt good at that moment but then, a couple of minutes later, regretted it as not a good choice?

Can you picture your future self, say, you in two months? What will probably be the same? What might be different? What might happen between now and then that will change your circumstances?

Activity

This is based on the 10-10-10 exercise advocated by Suzy Welch.

Think of a choice you want to make. For each option try to picture your life going in a direction. Then fill in table 2.2. An example is provided.

Table 2.2. 2-2-2 Exercise

Choice	*What My Life Will Be like Two Minutes after My Choice:*	*What My Life Will Be like Two Weeks after My Choice:*	*What My Life Will Be like Two Months after My Choice:*
Option A			
Option B			
Example Option A: Sign up to try out for a part in a play.	I would be excited but nervous.	If I am selected, I would be practicing in the play. I will be busier. I think it will be more work, but I will enjoy it.	I will be performing in the play by this time. I could have fun and people could clap for me.
Example Option B: Do nothing	There would be no change, but I'd be wondering if I still should do it.	There would be no change. I'd have more free time, but I may wonder what it would have been like if I did it.	I'd have free time, but I may attend the play and wonder or regret that I didn't sign up.

Follow-Up Questions/Discussions

Does considering your choice in three different time frames change your opinion of the choice?

Does one option get better over time and one get worse? How can this help you choose?

We have only taken this out to two months. What kind of choices need even more time to see how the choice of paths go in different directions and take you to different places?

Part of the problem is that we can't be sure what might happen in the future. We can see that some choices, however, increase the likelihood of good and bad things happening as a result of our choice (being in better shape for the sports season or having more or less money). How can you better account for a choice likely leading to other things down the road?

As people look at how each option affects them, some people see the more immediate effects as emotional ones (happy) and the longer effects as practical (I will be better/worse off). Did you find that? How can you balance immediate emotion with what is practical in the long term? How do great athletes or artists do it?

Chapter Three

Nonrational Factors in Choosing

Let me tell you about our morning ritual. What we have done first thing on every morning, going back years, has been to feed the cats, scoop the litter, and take care of our feline lords' and ladies' needs before we started attending to our own. It hasn't mattered if it's a weekday or a weekend. It hasn't changed by whether we have work or the day off or how we have felt. We walk from the bedroom to the front of the house, past the coffee maker, and open the big wooden window blinds. "Cat TV" is then on, and so our furry three have been able to get in some early birdwatching before they settle in for their midmorning nap.

We occasionally ask ourselves why we do this ritual. In the end, though, we wouldn't want it any other way, and we will continue to do so. We like our feline furry friends. It's our choice. It's just not a rational one.[1]

In the last chapter, we explained the way we all make—or at least should make—rational choices: by considering and comparing costs and benefits. That's what the field of economics studies. Unfortunately, that's not what humans always do. In fact, noted economist Richard Thaler—you'll hear a lot more about him next chapter—says that there are two kinds of people, "econs," who live in the world of economic theory and who always do the rational thing, and "humans" who are, well, pretty much the rest of us in the nontheoretical world of textbooks.[2]

Being human means having emotions, likes, and dislikes for no reason we can state. We have moods that change the way we look at things. It sounds chaotic, even negative, but these emotional bents, our unexplainable preferences, are the spice that make life fun, exciting, and flavorful. In the old TV and movie franchise *Star Trek*, there was a planet called Vulcan on which the people there eliminated (as much as they could) all emotion. They forged ahead in science and were always logical in their choices. While viewers admired Vulcans, very few in fact wanted to live like them.[3]

So for all that we know, our tending to our cats uses up our limited resources of time and pre-coffee energy that we may need to get to writing and other chores, but we spend the time taking care of them. We are crazy cat people, and we own it. (See lesson 3.1.)

Everyone has choices that they can't rationally justify and yet will stick with.

Neat, rationally aligned cost-benefit charts become skewed by our emotions and preferences. These skewed feelings may not be specifically *quantifiable*, but if economists want to study more accurately how people choose, they need to take these factors into account. (See lesson 3.2.)

Welcome to *behavioral economics*. It is a relatively new field where psychology, the study of the human mind and behavior, intersects with economics, the study of choice. It seeks to look at all the factors that guide us in choosing between options, including factors which are *conscious* or *subconscious*, rational or *nonrational*, and quantifiable or not. We prefer the term *nonrational* over *irrational* when discussing factors in choosing. Irrational implies it is a bad factor, even possibly a rejection of rational factors, often leading to bad choices. Not all choices based on nonrational, emotional factors are bad—think of choices based on love. So to distinguish those motivators from rational ones, we use nonrational.

In many ways the growth of behavioral economics is part of a newly popular academic approach called interdisciplinary studies.[4] Students sometimes ask, "Why do I study math, then science, then English, when in reality, the real world doesn't separate them and I have to use all of them in combination?" The student is right on this point, as he needs English to understand the math problem, math to quantify his measurements in the science lab, and even science to help explain why the characters' reactions in the story were very human. Schools separate subjects so that one field of study can be emphasized more at a time. It's like a martial arts student who works on punches in some classes, kicks in another, blocking in a third, and movement in a fourth. Once the student enters the actual sparring ring, everything is needed at the same time.

Take the problem of pollution. We need science to measure it and see the bad effects. But if everyone knows pollution is bad, why do people still pollute? We need sociology to study how the way people live causes a pollution problem and psychology to understand how to get people to feel more individually responsible to take care of it. Eventually, we will need the field of the government to try to find a solution, who will be working with economics to make sure the measures are affordable.

Let's get back to behavioral economics specifically; some might say it was one of the first interdisciplinary fields.[5] Thorstein Veblen was an economist at the turn of the twentieth century. He initially had many of the same ideas as other economists, that the study of choice selection was best limited to rational factors. The apocryphal story goes that his eyes were opened when he was relaxing in a park and noticed how many wealthy men walked around using fancy walking sticks even though they didn't seem to need them to help walk. He also noticed that the wealthy buy and show off a lot of stuff that they didn't really need, such as overly fancy silk top hats and bigger-than-they-needed horse-drawn carriages:[6] These people were good with money, yet they seemed to waste a lot of it in public. Their choices didn't appear rational.

Veblen decided that no matter how money smart these people were, they were still human and had a nonrational side. He concluded that people don't like to just have wealth; they want to show it off. He called it *conspicuous consumption*, or the act of openly spending money, even wasting it, so other people would be impressed or jealous.[7]

Over 120 years later, Veblen's ideas still hold true. Change out the silk top hats with the latest fashion craze or the oversized horse carriage with a luxury car, and people are still doing conspicuous consumption.

If one thing has changed, it's that people are getting their ideas about what to irrationally buy from mass media. Many check out the famous influencers to gauge what "rich" and "successful" look like so we can imitate them. We also want to blend in with and bond with our friends by often tapping into the latest trend. We don't want to miss out or be labeled as odd, and we fear people may judge us. We seek to show our individuality in the same way everyone else is doing it. (See lesson 3.3.)

What became apparent to people studying choice making, people like us, was a way to intersect behavioral economics, which is already interdisciplinary, with a study of media and how it influences us and our choice selection. That mixture arose in the 1990s and is called *media literacy*.[8] The goal of media literacy is not to tell a consumer to buy or not buy something or to agree or disagree with what they read in a text or a book. It is politically neutral. Rather, like Veblen, media literacy wants to make people aware of all the factors that can affect them when they are exposed to media—the rational and nonrational, conscious and subconscious, and intentional and accidental ones. It's not even just about the content or message but understanding the impact of the delivery system itself, from a book to the TV to the internet. Then potential consumers can choose which of those factors they wish to include in their cost-benefit calculations and which to exclude. They then can make the best choice for themselves. (See lesson 3.4.)

Finally, there is one last part of media literacy that addresses messaging beyond the consumption of goods, or things outside of ourselves. Media also messages regarding many aspects of our individual identities. We have summarized those aspects as each person's "Holy GRAILS."[9] Some of these aspects are changeable as we better discover who we are, some change naturally over time, and others we cannot change. However they exist, media sends messages regarding each aspect that tells people what that aspect should mean for them and how they should be. The messages can be confusing, especially for a young person just coming into seeing him- or herself by that aspect and who is starting to self-define. Media literacy, again, does not tell a person they must accept or reject any particular message about who they are. It seeks, rather, to empower youth to be able to understand the messages communicated, shown, or otherwise implied to them. The young person then has more control and self-determination as to who they are and want to be, exercised by their own "Yes, please" or "No, thank you." (See lesson 3.5.)

NOTES

1. We even hauled our menagerie across the Atlantic to live with us in Spain and then hauled them all back—plus an additional one—when we returned. Twenty-four hours of travel with listening to the howls of one particular unhappy cat reinforced the irrationality of our choices.

2. David Henderson, "Richard H. Thaler," Econlib, accessed December 26, 2022. https://www.econlib.org/library/Enc/bios/Thaler.html.

3. The series would occasionally have episodes where Spock, the Vulcan science and first officer, had to take command of the ship. He was capable but not as capable as Captain Kirk, the human ship captain who would tap into his passion, intuition, and even irrationality to save the day.

4. Allen F. Repko, Rick Szostak, and Michelle Phillips Buchberger, *Introduction to Interdisciplinary Studies* (Los Angeles: Sage, 2017). Combining academic fields is not a new technique. What is new is the advent of it as an intentional and formal method or approach, witnessed by the rise in universities of specific departments dedicated to the approach.

5. For a more detailed evolution of the field of behavioral economics, see Jim Wasserman and David W. Loveland, *Middle Schoolers, Meet Media Literacy* (Lanham, MD: Rowman & Littlefield, 2019). Here we provide just a short summary.

6. The Vanderbilt family home, Biltmore, was completed in 1895. The 250-room French Renaissance chateau includes 35 bedrooms, 43 bathrooms, and 65 fireplaces.

7. Veblen had a lot more interesting ideas and examples. A wooden spoon does the same job as a silver one, is cheaper, and requires less upkeep. Yet people desire the silver one.

8. *Media literacy* as a term is still being defined. One often finds it used in very different ways in academia and education. For example, while we use it as a study of messaging, others use it as a term for instruction in how to use media, such as in the technical aspects of making a podcast.

9. Jim Wasserman, *High Schoolers, Meet Media Literacy* (Lanham, MD: Rowman & Littlefield, 2019). GRAILS is an acronym for gender, race (and ethnicity), age, income, lifestyle, and sexuality. We understand that there are other aspects of identity that are layered within these groups or even exist beyond them. Again, our goal is to create a more simplified framework—at the risk of a bit of incompleteness—to make it more easily presentable to youth as one of their first introductions to the topic. Please feel free to tweak as desired—and let us know!

Chapter 3 Accompanying Lessons

LESSON 3.1. THINKING ABOUT NOT THINKING

Focus of Exploration

Nonrational choice selection.

Intro Questions / Thoughts for Students

Do you ever go on autopilot, going about your day making choices without really thinking about it? When are you more likely to be on autopilot? Does it depend on the circumstances (familiar choices versus being in a strange situation), time of day (morning versus evening), or with certain people (parents versus friends)?

When are you more likely to make choices based on your emotions or how you feel at that moment versus thinking logically about the pros and cons for each choice?

Activity

For an hour, try to be self-aware about all the choices you make. You can also do this with a friend so you can help each other keep watch over each other. As you go about, use table 3.1.

Table 3.1. Tracking What Made Me Choose, with Example (Expand Table as Needed)

Time (About)	Where Are You	Choice You Had to Make	Special Circumstances	Used More Reason or Emotion or "Just 'Cause" to Choose	Other Observations
Example: 4:30 p.m.	Grocery store	What should I buy for an afternoon snack—chips or carrots?	I am very tired from staying up late and very hungry.	I worked hard last night, and I deserve my favorite potato chips!	I know it is not healthy, but a little bit of chips won't hurt. I will eat healthier next time.

Follow-Up Questions/Discussions

Which were easier to notice, choices you made based on reason, emotion, or "just 'cause"? Which were the hardest to be self-aware about? Why do you think that is?

Did you see any patterns as to which kinds of choices were based on emotion and which on reason or "just 'cause"?

Did you find any choices that you thought were based on one of the three categories, but as you thought about it more, you realized that a lot of your choices were based on something else?

LESSON 3.2. APPEALS WITH APPEAL

Focus of Exploration

Being aware of how you react to appeals.

Intro Questions / Thoughts for Students

When do emotional appeals work better on you to get you to do or choose something, and when do appeals based on reason work better to persuade you?

Activity

Movies and even short videos try to move or persuade viewers. Part of a movie critic's job is to evaluate and rate how successful a film is at doing that (do you buy in?).

Watch a video online, especially one that is asking you to do something or move you. Watch whether they give you reasons, such as facts, or try to appeal to your feelings and emotions (like not feeling left out, wanting to look cool or happy, or wanting to help others in sympathy). Write a critique or review, like a movie reviewer, of the video and how it tried to appeal to you. Include the following:

- What it is they want you to do.
- What do they say to try to get you to do it? What techniques were used to move or persuade you, like certain shots, statistics, or music?
- Are the appeals more to your reason or emotion?
- As a reviewer, how many stars from one (poor) to five (great) do you give to their appeal and its effectiveness?

For rating how much the appeal persuades you, rank it from one (doesn't work on me at all) to five (it makes me really want to do it).

Follow-Up Questions/Discussions

Which appeals seemed to work better on you, appeals to your reason or emotion? Did it depend on what they wanted you to do? Why?

Did you find some videos use all reason or all emotion rather than an even mix? What kinds tend to heavily use more reason, and which use more emotion?

Many people say they feel moved by another's passion, that they feel the emotion of another like it is contagious. Does that happen to you? When? Does that also happen with reason?

Having watched a video of someone you don't know personally to evaluate how they try to appeal to you, try watching people you know, like friends or family. See if they use more reason or emotion, and note when they do use each in trying to persuade you.

LESSON 3.3. THING FOR THE BLING

Focus of Exploration

Conspicuous consumption.

Intro Questions / Thoughts for Students

We mostly obtain things because they are useful or make us happy (which is a kind of usefulness). Do you have anything where part of its usefulness is that people admire, even like you more, because they know you have it?

Have you ever shown off that you have something so that people will admire you for it?

Activity

Look around your home and make a list of items that give you or a family member internal happiness because you personally like having it (as much or more than for its practical usefulness) or external happiness because people admire or like you more for having it (called *bling*). Also, look at picture posts on social media or videos online, and see if you can spot any bling the person in the video shows or mentions (like taking an expensive vacation). Some things can be both, such as a trophy that makes the owner proud that she won it and is displayed to impress others.

Follow-Up Questions/Discussions

Internal happiness and external bling aren't just for things. It can also be for activities. Can you think of anything that is done where a large part of what the participant likes about it is that people know they do it, like play a sport or are in a play?

Since bling's main value is to make the owner feel good—either in showing it off or just in having it—how can we decide if it is worth the cost to buy it? Did you ever spend money or effort to get something and then didn't feel as good having it as you thought you would? What if you bought something to impress others, and they weren't impressed? Is it better to buy things because they make us happy and to not care what others think?

External bling is to impress others, which also may make others feel bad because they don't have it. How far is it OK to do before it is too much bragging?

Have you ever felt bad because it seems like others have more bling than you? There is an expression that says "Don't compare your daily documentary to someone else's highlight reel." What do you think that means?

LESSON 3.4. STRENGTHENING WEAK KNEES

Focus of Exploration

Identifying persuasive emotional appeals.

Intro Questions / Thoughts for Students

For your family or friends, do you know what kind of emotional or nonrational appeals work on them? Does it win them over if you tell them one choice will be funny or make them popular or even that you will like them more? Maybe they can be persuaded by your telling them that they will have a greater sense of satisfaction or feel good about themselves? Maybe you know that the person you are trying to appeal to softens to pictures of cute puppies or kittens?

Do you know which emotional appeals work best on you? How can you recognize when you are being persuaded by that kind of appeal, and when is it OK to let yourself be persuaded by that?

Activity

First, list out what kinds of emotional (nonrational) appeals you think work best on you. List not only the kind of emotion, like wanting to be loved, cool, or popular, but also what pictures make you go weak in the knees. Maybe there's a song that moves you too.

Now, find an ad or video that uses those kinds of appeals that get to you.

- How does the ad use that appeal to get you to want or do something?
- Does the appeal directly relate to the topic—like a kitten as part of a pitch to adopt animals, or is it unnecessary (*gratuitous*), such as an ad for cookies that has kittens?

Follow-Up Questions/Discussions

Of course it's OK to want to do something for nonrational reasons, but when is it too much? When should you check your emotions and try to think rationally? When should you check your rational thinking and just let your emotions, especially positive ones like love, guide you?

Are there any emotions or feelings that should not be worked to get someone to choose something? Is it OK to make someone angry or scared to persuade them to do something?

If you wanted to prevent another person from falling under the control of an emotional appeal you thought was wrong, what would you say to them? Would that strategy work for you?

LESSON 3.5. JUST LIKE ME... ONLY, NOT

Focus of Exploration

Stereotypes.

Intro Questions / Thoughts for Students

We tend to sort things into categories to make things easier to understand, like fruits versus vegetables. However, can we do this too much? What is the possible problem of overgrouping things as alike? Maybe ask a tomato.

Have you ever thought that because something reminds you of something else, the two things must be the same? Have you ever thought that two people who you thought were alike in one way must be the same in other ways? Have you ever assumed that because someone reminds you of someone else, they must act or think the same way or like and dislike the same things?

Activity

Fill in the following for yourself:

My gender is _____.
My race and/or ethnicity is _____.
I am ____ years old.
I live in _____ city or state.
My favorite things to do are _____.

Now, for as many as you can, go on to an internet browser, and do an image search for "typical _____" with one of your responses in the blank. Look at the pictures, and ask yourself how the pictures you see are like you but also different from you.

Follow-Up Questions/Discussions

When we create broad descriptions or ideas about groups of people, they are called *stereotypes*. They can give a broad, general picture, like taking a satellite picture of the Earth. The satellite picture won't capture all the variations of high mountains to low valleys. In the same way, a stereotype about a group of people will not capture all the variations within the group.

Do you feel the pictures for a "typical" person like you are accurate? Do they capture the wide variety of people in that group? Do they capture you? How is this so and not so?

If stereotypes relating to you may not be accurate, what about stereotypes you see or hear about groups different from you? What groups can you think of like that?

Some people justify a stereotype by saying they know some people of that group who are like that. Is that a good argument? Would that work for groups you belong to? Why or why not?

Are stereotypes that don't upset you OK, like assuming you are good at something because of a stereotype about your group? Why or why not?

Bonus exploratory on stereotypes: Under the *all* category (to get words and not just pictures), type in "Why do [one of your responses]" and then stop typing. Most search engines, like Google, have an autocomplete feature that suggests how to finish that search. The suggested endings to that question are suggested because they are the most common finishers of that sentence, especially in your area and demographics, so the search engine is guessing it is the rest of your question. You can see what the most common questions are about your group. Do you do what they are asking about for your group? Do you feel like the questions are good ones or based on stereotypes or even bad information? If you saw questions based on stereotypes about your groups that aren't true, what things that you think are true for groups you don't belong to might be wrong?

Chapter Four

Nudges, or External Factors on Our Choices

So far, we've taken the outwardly simple moment of choice making and seen how the inner workings, like in a watch or phone, can be complicated. You are in a store and hungry, so you go to the chip aisle. There are so many choices. The rational part of your brain likes the lower price of one. The nonrational part of you is tempted by the bright red "Extreme hotness!" label to see if your mouth can handle it. As they say in advertising, however, "But wait, there's more!"

You eye a certain brand, Free-Toes (with an extra-hot-spice version called Toe-Nail!), but realize it's way on the top shelf and would require a jump and strain to get it, and you may even have to embarrassingly ask someone to get it for you. On the other hand, a brand you like (but not quite as much), Dori's-Toes, is right there at face level. You take the easy way out and choose the chips within reach.

In behavioral economics, that's called a *nudge*.

In the last section, we mentioned Richard Thaler. A pioneer in behavioral economics, he was the person who distinguished between econs, theoretical people who always do the rational thing in economic theory, and humans, real people who sometimes do things for nonrational reasons.

Thaler also popularized the word *nudge*. Outside of economics, a nudge is an outside force that gently gets you to change what you are doing or to go in a different direction. You don't see the mess on the sidewalk in front of you, but a friend points it out or slightly bumps you, and you walk around the mess. Or maybe you are not paying attention in a meeting or class, and your friend makes a sound to tell you people are looking at you. It's not a shove, as you still have a choice, but there is a clearly preferred choice the nudger wants you to make.

In the same way, Thaler's behavioral economics nudge is a suggestion or emphasis for choosing choice B over choice A. Nudges don't make you choose option B, but they set up the choice so option B is given advantages to be chosen over option A. Back in the chip example, it's up to you what to buy, but the extra effort required to jump and strain and maybe the fear of what others might think when seeing you can be enough of a nudge for you to choose the more easily accessible chips, especially if you are tired, in a hurry, or with others. That setup, intentional or not, was a nudge.

Nudges can be intentionally put in place or can be a matter of circumstance. There might be an accidental spill on the ground in front of some brands, and the store hasn't cleaned it up yet. By walking around the spill, you are accidentally nudged away from those unlucky brands.[1]

Nudgers who try to get you to choose option B over option A might think it's a better choice for the chooser's sake. Parents nudge their children to eat healthier by serving vegetables instead of french fries. Nudges can also be motivated because a choice is better for the nudgers. Fast-food restaurants often ask if you'd like fries or a drink with your burger because those items are more profitable for them.

These nudges seem small, but they work. A well-placed arrow pointing in a particular direction can get enough traffic going that way to make it worthwhile, whether it's chips at eye level or a pop-up on the screen saying to check out a website. The famous nineteenth-century showman P. T. Barnum had a problem with people taking so long to stroll through his museum that the line to get in was backing up. So Barnum put up pointers and signs in his museum: "This Way to the Egress!" People wanted to see what the signs were about, so they followed the nudge through doors . . . to the outside of his museum![2] Today people still follow nudges, such as the authors directing you to learn more about nudging by going to their previous books![3] (See lesson 4.1.)

Nudging works so well that behavioral economists are now hired to help set up the presentation of choices—called *choice architecture*—to nudge choosers a certain way. Richard Thaler discusses how putting fruit at the beginning of a cafeteria lunch line as a first choice, rather than at the end, increases students' eating healthier. People hesitant to choose can be nudged by adding a time element to the choice architecture. (See lesson 4.2.)

Your parents make all the choices for you when you are a baby. Then they start giving you options but often with heavy nudging. It can be as simple as a word or phrase such as, "You don't really want that yucky stuff, do you?" They ask their children if the chores are done as nudging reminders. *Presumptive choices* can be built in, such as telling a child he has the absolute choice to watch a movie, play a game, or read . . . after finishing his or her homework.[4] (See lesson 4.3.)

We like to think we choose our path, but the path also guides where we go. When you buy and first set up a computer, you will notice there's already an internet browser and many programs such as antivirus protection that the computer seller has thoughtfully preloaded for you, usually because they have a deal with that software supplier. You have to opt out to use something else and may do so. Many people, however, don't bother, as they are eager to get going. That is the power of *default choice architecture*—unless you say otherwise, you automatically go with their choice. It's harder to go look for another internet browser or virus protection, so many just use and stick with what's there. The software providers know this; that is why they provide the software initially. They also know that, after a year, when the antivirus pops up a warning to renew or be exposed to infection, many will just opt for renewal.

Default choice architecture is a popular way to nudge a person's choice because it is based on a simple human truth: no one likes extra work and many avoid it when they can. If you don't see any real problem, why do the extra work to find a possibly better option? (See lesson 4.4.)

The extra work we have to do to not take the default choice or to do anything extra is called a *transaction cost*. Transaction costs, small or large, can nudge us. We want a good, delicious meal, but the effort to plan it out and make it—thaw and cut up the chicken, chop up the vegetables, prepare the seasoning—is too much of a transaction cost. So we put it off until we are hungry, then settle for a basic sandwich or order pizza instead. Sometimes just focusing and thinking hard about our choices and the impact of each option is enough to make us just shrug and accept the default choice, whether it's the chef's recommendation on a menu, the featured item for sale on a website, or just checking "I agree" on the terms and conditions so as to move on.

The online world has had a tremendous effect on calculating transaction costs in choosing to do things, especially at the *buy-in point*. That's the cost to start the switch, like that moment you choose to get off the couch, change clothes, and go work out. Consider someone who has a momentary interest in a subject or hobby, whether it be about model airplanes, a conspiracy theory, or even a new way they see their own identity. Pre-internet, the person wanting to investigate further would have had to take the time and effort to go to a library. They would have had to spend money to buy magazines and other publications. If they wanted to find other people with a similar interest, they would have had to seek them out and find them, a difficult task in any case but especially in less populated areas. If the person's interest was frowned upon by society for good or bad reasons, the person would risk public embarrassment in seeking out information. All of that totals a high buy-in cost. With the internet, all these initial costs of time, money, effort, and risk are avoided, as the person can simply look into the topic from the privacy of their own home internet. This is much more affordable and enticing. (See lesson 4.5.)

All of these ideas about choice architecture to nudge a person can be found when you use your phone or computer. One example is the sea of little red dots by app icons that tell you there's a new message or update. Some people can ignore the red dots, but some just have to stop what they are doing and check out the cause of the cyber measles. That's a choice made as to where the person should focus one's time and attention. The choice, however, was nudged by the phone's design and notification settings. If a person rudely turns away in the middle of a real life conversation or, worse, looks away from the road while driving, it can have negative consequences. Still, it's generally to the app's benefit to have you use it,[5] so phone operating systems are designed to have these little nudges. In contrast, there is no built-in nudge that you are spending too much time on the phone or that your homework is due and you should put down the phone, so you have to counternudge yourself. You could go into the phone settings and turn off the red-dot reminders. That takes extra work, however, and as we said, that is a transaction cost. It is easier to tell yourself "I will just ignore the red dots when I need to" and then (Whoops!) get a message. "BRB." (See lesson 4.6.)

Speaking of transaction costs, have you ever noticed how often a video that you want to see online follows a quick ad by a sponsor or even a plug by someone in the video? Why are they so often at the front of the video? Well, watching those ads you aren't really interested in is a transaction cost, but the cost is worth it to see the content you want. If those ads and plugs were at the end, after you have already gotten the content, then the transaction cost would not be worth it, like a food stand giving you the choice to make a donation after you got the food rather than charging you before you get it. Fewer people would do it, and as we said, sites and video makers get paid by the eyeballs on the ads.[6] You could jump ahead in the video to the content you want, but again, you'd have to move around to find it, so the transaction cost is too high. So you "choose" to watch the front-end ads, the presumptive choice set up that way by the site.[7] (See lessons 4.7 and 4.8.)

NOTES

1. Thaler mainly addresses intentional nudges, as he focuses on *choice architecture*, or how choices can be set up to send people in a direction for their choices. For many, however, especially youth, nudges can be the result of life's serendipity.

2. Egress is another word for exit.

3. For a more complete discussion of nudging, we suggest you check out Jim Wasserman and David W. Loveland, *Middle Schoolers, Meet Media Literacy* (Lanham, MD: Rowman & Littlefield, 2019).

4. One of our sons, when young and coming in happily dirty from playing outside, loved having the apparent autonomy when we told him, "It's completely *your* choice: you can take your bath right now either upstairs or downstairs."

5. Apps often get advertising money based on how many people use their app and how long they stay on it.

6. Sites monitor when people stop watching.

7. This tactic is certainly not new to online videos. Television shows often began with a message from their sponsor. They might also start with a short, dramatic opening scene or *grabber*, then go to opening credits and a first round of ads before returning to finish the grabber scene and continue the story.

Chapter 4 Accompanying Lessons

LESSON 4.1. NUDGE AND BUDGE, BUT DON'T HOLD A GRUDGE

Focus of Exploration

Recognizing *nudges* in one's choice, *stakeholders* in a choice.

Intro Questions / Thoughts for Students

When you are making a choice, do people try to persuade you to go one way or the other? Do they ever do it indirectly, like dropping hints or portraying one choice as better?

When you have a choice, do you consider *stakeholders*, or all the people besides yourself who will benefit or lose out by your choice? Do stakeholders ever try to influence your choices?

Activity

Think of a choice you will need to make in the near future, such as what to order at a restaurant. As you go into your choice, watch for attempted nudges on your decision. You might prompt them by asking aloud "What shall I have?" If you are planning on observing your parents or friends, you need to *not* let them know they are part of the observation.

Look for nudges of the following different kinds:

- How are your choices presented and in what order? Are some highlighted?
- What words, even suggestions, are used for each choice?
- Are there personal recommendations, such as "I like X" or "The X looks good!"?
- Is there any hedging of "your" choice, such as "It's up to you, but I think the X is a good choice"?
- Are there any visuals, such as on the menu, that seem to emphasize one choice?
- Are the advantages or disadvantages of a choice presented to you?

Follow-Up Questions/Discussions

Do you notice that certain people or things, such as parents or menus, tend to have common techniques of nudging? Do they have go-tos like "It's healthy!" that they tend to use often?

Some nudges are so built in and subtle that they are hard to detect, like a friend saying "Cool!" when you say you're thinking about choosing one option. Nudges also don't have to be intentional to work, but they can still nudge you toward a choice, especially if it's the popular one. Even a smile or nodding of the head can be a nudge. How many unintended nudges can you find?

We said above that if you were going to include your parents or friends in your observation, it was important to not let them know they were being observed. Why do you think that is? Do you change how you act when you know you are being observed? How do you think social scientists keep their subjects from knowing what is being tested or observed?

Let's reverse the situation to when someone else is the chooser and *you* are the stakeholder affected by their choice—such as a friend choosing what you two will do that day. What are your go-to nudges? How far can you nudge someone before it is too much and you are not letting your friend choose for him- or herself?

LESSON 4.2. NOW OR NEVER

Focus of Exploration

Nudge by time restriction and/or pressure.

Intro Questions / Thoughts for Students

Do you ever feel pressured to make a choice right away? Have you ever felt pressured but didn't see why you had to choose so quickly?

Are you the kind of person who reacts to "Hurry up!" encouragement, or do you not change speed so much?

Activity

Look for ads, recommendations, offers, and nudges that suggest you must act quickly or that there is only a limited time to respond:

- It uses phrases like "Limited time!" or "Offer expires soon."
- It uses direct encouragement with phrases like "Hurry!" and "Act now!" (and lots of exclamation points!).
- It uses an indirect time limitation because supplies are limited, or they may say, "If you don't take it, I will ask someone else if they want it."

Follow-Up Questions/Discussions

For the nudges you found, was the time limit logical—such as acting before the holiday is over? Were there time limits that seemed to be for no reason except that the nudger wanted a quick answer? Does that make a difference in how much the hurrying nudged you?

Did you ever resent being hurried into choosing? Does it ever make you push back by intentionally not hurrying or even rejecting the offer? Why is that? What can you do when you feel unnecessarily hurried to choose or feel uncomfortable making a choice right away?

Do you agree with the saying "If it is a good deal today, it will be a good deal tomorrow"? When is that not the case for you?

Are the time nudges online the same as time nudges IRL? Do you think your sense of time is different online than IRL?

LESSON 4.3 AN OFFER YOU CAN'T REFUSE

Focus of Exploration:

Presumptive and *pretend choice* architecture.

Intro Questions / Thoughts for Students

When someone comes to you to offer a choice rather than you going to them, how do they introduce the choices? Have you ever been presented a choice, but the options are already limited?

Have you ever had someone offer you a *pretend choice*, where they try to make it look like you have a choice, but the choices are so lopsided or they amount to the same thing that you don't really have a choice, or as is said in the movie *The Godfather*, they have "an offer [you] can't refuse?"

Activity

Look for situations where you are presented with a *presumptive* or *pretend choice*:

- It is an unexpected choice, where the presenter suggests things you didn't ask for.
- It is where you don't have the option to not choose and "walk away."
- The costs and benefits of the options are so imbalanced, there really is no logical reason to choose one option.
- The presenter of the choices is heavily signaling, emphasizing, or telling you in other ways what "your" choice should be.

Follow-Up Questions/Discussions

When we look at these things about how a choice is set up, especially if it is done so to nudge you toward a particular choice, it is called *choice architecture*. What does the word architect or architecture imply to you? How are house architects and choice architects similar in what they design?

Are there particular circumstances or certain people you're with where you find more occasions of presumptive or pretend choices offered? Why do you think that is?

Why do people pretend to offer you a choice rather than just tell you what they want you to do? Would you rather people say "I want you to do this"? When is that?

Sometimes, the choice architecture to nudge you can simply be by the order of the choices. Sometimes, the choice architect's preference is given first, so nothing looks good afterward. Sometimes, the choice they want you to make is offered last in order to look like the one good option after bad ones. Can you think of cases of both?

Do you ever offer a presumptive or pretend choice to someone? When? Is that OK?

LESSON 4.4. NOT YOUR DEFAULT

Focus of Exploration

Default choice architecture.

Intro Questions / Thoughts for Students

Have you ever realized you must choose to act in order to change things to be how you wanted?

Have you ever had someone say "If you don't choose, you get X"?

Have you ever been offered something you didn't want, but you didn't opt out because you were afraid of how you might look in turning it down?

Activity

Look for situations where a specific choice will be made for you unless you choose otherwise.

Follow-Up Questions/Discussions

A choice that will happen or be made for you if you do nothing is called a *default choice*. Are there particular circumstances or particular people with whom you find more default choices?

Sometimes default choices arise from group pressure, such as when your friends say, "We are all going to do this unless you have a problem with it." It's hard to speak up, but what are some things you could say or do in that situation?

A famous quote—attributed to many different people—is "The only thing necessary for the triumph of evil is that good men do nothing." What do you think that means? How does it relate to default choices? How does that relate to your life?

LESSON 4.5. YOU ARE FREE TO CHOOSE, BUT IT'S GONNA COST YOU

Focus of exploration

Transaction costs, buy-in point, benefit ratio.

Intro Questions / Thoughts for Students

Have you ever thought about changing a choice, but you just went with the way things were because it was too hard to put in the effort or time to change things, even though you liked the alternative more than what you were doing?

In physics, *inertia* is an object's tendency to keep doing what it's doing. If it's not moving, it tends to continue to not move. Have you ever felt inertia when thinking about making a change in your life?

Activity

Look for choices you have where there is a default choice (what happens if you don't do anything) but that you can change by choosing something else.

For each choice change, rate the benefit (B) of changing to the new choice on a scale of one (no benefit) to five (extreme benefit). Similarly, rate the cost, including the effort (C) of changing your choice from one (no cost) to five (extreme cost or risk). Divide B/C to generate a *benefit ratio*.

Follow-Up Questions/Discussions

The benefit-ratio score can range from .2 (1 benefit/5 cost) to 5 (5 benefit/1 cost). A benefit ratio of one means the benefits and costs are the same. A benefit ratio below one indicates costs outweigh benefits, and a benefit ratio over one indicates benefits outweigh costs. Rank your choice changes by their benefit ratio, from highest to lowest. Do the numbers seem to reflect how you would actually feel about changing? Where is your not-worth-it-to-change line?

Did you ever feel like a choice architect who says you can change has intentionally made the transaction cost high? Maybe they seem to put in or emphasize extra costs to dissuade you, such as telling you that people will not like you as much if you change your mind.

Transaction costs are usually short-term, while often, the gain from changing is long-term. Many people don't make a change because the first step is so costly, the initial *buy-in point*. It's like that first effort to get off the couch, even if you are going to do something fun. Eating healthy may not be as tasty in the short term, but you are healthier in the long term. How can you keep your eyes on the prize for a great long-term gain to work past short-term transaction costs and get past the initial buy-in point? Some people put up a picture of their goal or of someone they admire who achieved the long-term goal, or they put regular reminders on a calendar. What can you do? Can you also factor in the long-term bad effects of not changing choices, like regret?

LESSON 4.6. ALARMING NEWS

Focus of Exploration

Interrupting nudges, alarms, and alerts.

Intro Questions / Thoughts for Students

Alarms are designed to be instant nudges because they warn you of something important, like danger. Have you ever experienced an alarm? How did you react?

One step that is less immediate from "alarms" are "alerts," which let you know something is happening that you might want to know about or is waiting for you.

Activity

For one day, try to observe and list all the alarms and alerts that are around you. They can be fire alarms, signs telling you to watch out, or someone telling you something. Note and then rank each on how important is your need to immediately be warned for your health and safety, from one (not very much, such as a posted text from your friend about a cool show to watch) to five (very much, like a bad storm in the area). Also rank in the same one-to-five way how personally important it is for you. For example, your life may not depend on knowing your friend responded to a text, but it is still important to you that she got your message. Use table 4.1.

Table 4.1. Rating the DI Factor of Alarms and Alerts (Expand Table as Needed)

Notification	How Necessary Is It That You Know About It Immediately (N)?	How Important to You Is It That You Know About It Immediately (I)?	Multiply N and I For The DI (Don't Ignore!) Factor.

Follow-Up Questions/Discussions

Ranking what you found by the DI factors from highest to lowest, do you see any patterns?

Can some notice types be subdivided? Is a text from a parent the same as a text from a friend, or maybe it changes at a different time of day? If necessary, revise your chart to be more precise. Revising things as you consider them more deeply is an important part of being a social scientist.

Is there a predominant color or a sound used with alarms? Why do you think that is?

In the story of the boy who cried wolf, the youth sounds the wolf alarm just for his own amusement and pays a price. Do you know people who do this? Are stores that say "Sale ending now!" the same? Why or why not?

Are you over notified? Alarms and alerts take away from one of your most precious resources: your attention. How can you get control so that you have better choice over what you are alerted to and what are real alarms worthy of your attention? Phones and computers allow you some control over alerts and notifications in their settings, such as turning off some notifications. What else can you do? Some people are so overalarmed and -alerted that they just start ignoring all such warnings. Have you ever done that? Is that a good strategy?

People also talk about alarms and alerts going off in their head (like Spider-Man's Spider-Sense). What does that mean? Do you have internal alarms and alerts? When do you use them? When should you listen to them?

Do you create self-alerts, such as timer or calendar reminders? What are the benefits of using them? Where would they be on your DI scale?

LESSON 4.7. PLUGGED UP

Focus of Exploration

Placement of ads and promotional messaging, plugs.

Intro Questions / Thoughts for Students

For any movies and videos that you like, do you like the ads that come with it, especially before the video? What do you like about the ads? What do you not like?

Do you ever notice in videos that the person talking sometimes puts in a *plug* by mentioning a product or brand or telling you about something coming up? What about asking you to subscribe or even "like" the video? Do you mind these breaks in the content?

Activity

Watch videos or movies, and as you do, take note of promotions in and outside of content. Mark the time it occurs within the video as well as whether it is outside-content ads (like an ad by an outsider that pops up or interrupts the show) or an in-content plug (said by the person in the video, such as "Check out my other videos" or "Like this video down below" or even "Check out this stuff for sale"). Finally, mark how much you mind it from one (not much at all) to five (I *really* wish I didn't have to see it). Use table 4.2.

Table 4.2. Promos and Plugs (Expand Table as Needed)

Time in Video	Promotion	In (Plug) or Outside (Ad) of Content	How Much You Mind It from 1–5

Follow-Up Questions/Discussions

Did you find more plugs or ads? Which were harder to catch or to realize were promotions? Do you mind ads or plugs more? Why do you think that is?

Ads often are earlier in the video and plugs, later. Why do you think that is?

Is it OK for someone to pay a content creator or video host to do a plug if they think you'll not notice the plug but be nudged by it? When is it too much plugging or self-promotion? Would you take money to secretly plug stuff to friends? When would that be OK, and when wouldn't it be OK?

Are you OK with both plugs and ads because you are used to them? Ask adults what they think. Many years ago, movies in theaters did not have ads for products such as soft drinks before movies—just trailers for other movies. When the ads first started, people objected or said they disliked them. Now people accept them without thinking. Why is there the change?

Some streaming services allow users to pay more to *not* receive ads. That way, the streaming service either gets paid by the advertiser or the watcher, but they still get paid. How much would you pay to *not* watch ads before videos?

LESSON 4.8. WAR OF THE WORLDS

Focus of Exploration

Nudges IRL and online.

Intro Questions / Thoughts for Students

Now that you are an expert on nudges, do you see or feel like there is a difference between nudges on your choices IRL and online? How is it different? Is it in the type of nudging? Who is nudging you? What are they trying to get you to choose?

Activity

Choose something you are nudged about a lot. It can be some choice you make, such as what to do in your free time, what you should wear or do (What's cool?), what values you should have (What does an admirable person look like?), or something else. For this choice, look at how you are nudged to make that choice IRL. How do people you interact with face-to-face promote a certain choice or nudge you? How are ads or signs designed in terms of length, structure, colors, sounds, and the things they say to nudge you? How do institutions, like your school, set things up to nudge your choice, and how do they promote one choice or another? What is the *choice architecture* IRL designed to nudge you? In looking, consider the following:

- What are the options presented to me? Are there other options not offered?
- What is the option that I feel nudged toward in this choice?
- Who are the nudgers? Are they friends, people in authority I know, or even celebrities?
- What do the nudgers say or do to nudge me?
- Do they appeal to my emotion or reason more? How?
- How do the nudgers use nonverbal things like colors, sounds, facial expressions, and other nonwords to influence me?

Now, for that same choice, what messages and nudges do you see online about it? Does online nudging mainly agree or disagree with the choice promoted IRL? What is the choice architecture for online, and what techniques do nudgers on the internet use? Make a chart comparing the two.

Follow-Up Questions/Discussions

There was probably a mixture of nudges to all choices in both worlds, but did you see one kind of choice more heavily promoted in one world or the other? If so, why do you think each world promotes and nudges that choice?

Remember, analyzing data is only as good as the data you get, so get a wide variety and as much as you can from each world. Judging IRL by just your parents, for one example, may not be enough (called a *sampling error*). Also, be careful not to go into collecting data already deciding what you will find. You'll tend to look for things that agree with what you concluded beforehand and even ignore what doesn't agree. This is called *confirmation bias*.

We talked before about *choice architecture*, how choices are set up or presented to you. The choices can be presented equally, or one choice may always be offered first to make it look better or worse. Do you find the choice architecture the same online and IRL? Try to think of a choice you are given in both worlds, and specifically look if the choice architecture is the same.

This is a big observation of two really big worlds. It helps, therefore, to collaborate or talk with other investigators as many social scientists do. They exchange their findings and then look for the big picture that comes from putting all their findings together, like a large jigsaw puzzle. Also, talk about your data with others, as even if they did not collect or directly observe, they might have a different take on what you've found.

You can't control all the nudges on your choices. Still, how can knowing about the nudges and being more aware of them help you to choose?

Chapter Five

Sway

However many kinds of nudges there are, one thing they all have in common is that they all influence at the moment of choice—that glorious, empowering second of frozen time when the camera swings 360 degrees around you as you are in total command of your destiny, the captain of your ship, deciding between the fates of . . . OK, sometimes it's just whether you'll have a one kind of chips or another.

What if, however, when you come to the moment of choice, it turns out you are already prone to prefer option A over option B? What if that preexisting preference you have when you arrive at choice time is not completely yours but has been slowly put into you over time by outside people and circumstances?

It sounds like the stuff of brainwashing and espionage fiction, but the fact is that it happens not just a lot but in most choices you make. The nudges at choice time may get you across the finish line of choice, but there were a lot of previous nudges maybe going back years before you came to the choice selection. Together, they have made you now more likely to choose option A over option B. For option B to win, it's got to come from behind with a whole lot of present nudges pushing it ahead.

Consider poet Robert Frost's famous poem "The Road Not Taken":[1]

> Two roads diverged in a yellow wood,
> And sorry I could not travel both
> And be one traveler, long I stood
> And looked down one as far as I could
> To where it bent in the undergrowth;

> Then took the other, as just as fair,
> And having perhaps the better claim,
> Because it was grassy and wanted wear;
> Though as for that the passing there
> Had worn them really about the same,
>
> And both that morning equally lay
> In leaves no step had trodden black.
> Oh, I kept the first for another day!
> Yet knowing how way leads on to way,
> I doubted if I should ever come back.
>
> I shall be telling this with a sigh
> Somewhere ages and ages hence:
> Two roads diverged in a wood, and I—
> I took the one less traveled by,
> And that has made all the difference.

The poem famously describes a moment when a traveler has to choose between two paths: one that is well-worn by many others or the other, overgrown from disuse. After considering, the narrator chooses the path that has been less traveled, the one that is less clear and perhaps even more uncertain and dangerous. The poem is seen as a metaphor for the many times when we have to choose between the path that most people take or choose to go a different way. It can apply to choosing what education or career course one wants, how one wants to live one's life, or even just what to wear.

Reading the poem, one gets the impression the traveler chose the less-traveled path because he was just that kind of person. Many people relate to the poem because they see themselves as "that kind of a person." They are the rebel, the outlaw, and the up-stream swimmer, or simply one who may say, "Sorry, I just don't want to do it that way and I'm OK with that." (See lesson 5.1.)

So how did our traveler in the poem and the people who relate to him get to be those kinds of people before they arrived at that moment of choice? A lot of it, of course, may be because of their nature. Some babies are curious crawlers who look everywhere. Others are happy to chill in their crib. Maybe it's also a lifetime of historic nudges that have been slowly shaping the person as they've grown, like the tiny drops of calcified water that, over time, create towering stalagmites. Together, they have all helped form the structure and determined in which direction and form the stalagmite has grown.

In the same way, what is important but often missed about the poem is the tacit pressure society has put on the traveler. There is no active nudge of one person standing at the split saying, "Choose this route." Rather, the influence comes from many past travelers who have worn down one path over time.

They didn't plan to influence others or even work together, but over time, the cumulative effect is a suggestion that sways a traveler's choice.

If you had been born in another city or country, how might you be different? What other foods might be your favorites? What sports teams would you root for?[2] It is strange to think about, but what aspects of your core personality would be the same and which parts might be different? (See lesson 5.2.)

It would be confusing to call these past influences nudges as well because, as we said, nudges are reserved for the outside influences at the moment of the choice. So we call these long-term influences *sways*. Sway is obviously not a new word, nor are we the first to introduce it as a term of art in behavioral economics.[3] Our use of sway is different, however, in that sways are the *cumulative influences* that have formed predispositions and preferences over the years. They can be good or bad, such as what is first evoked in the mind by the word *snack*. It could be carrot sticks or greasy chips. Whatever is first evoked, however, has the inside track into being selected, whether it is a type of food or a particular brand.

To be swayed generally is to be guided softly in a direction, like a gentle breeze making tree branches move. It's not too forceful and, like the wind, is invisible. Still, we can see the wind's effects as things respond to it or we feel it.[4] Put another way, nudges tend to invoke an image of a person choosing whether to turn right or left, like a car at an intersection. Sways, however, gently cause the person to head in a direction over a period of time, like a boat tacking with the wind in its sails. (See lesson 5.3.)

No peeking, but clear your mind for a moment (except, of course, for reading this). Now, don't think too long, just go with your gut and picture or say out loud the first thing that comes to your mind when we say *candy bar*.

Got it? Ours is chock-o-cricks, the crunchy and smooth taste of crickets hand-dipped in chocolate.[5] Now, we would immediately say we chose chock-o-cricks because of the taste. Looking into our brains, however, we might see a lifetime of sways. There was a favorite uncle who gave them to us when we read together, or it was what we ate with the team as a snack after games. The color of the wrapper appeals to us and reminds us of how chock-o-cricks sponsored our favorite sports team or entertainment program. There was even a game we played based on collecting the cricket parts. We liked the slogan "The trick with the crick is to crunch and then munch!" And we have the jingle stuck in our heads.

All these sways can tilt the scales when choice time comes, even years later. Some, like toys with logos, were intended to make us feel positive seeing the brand early and maybe to influence a future choice. Others, like our favorite relative or admired friend liking the candy, weren't intentionally meant to sway us. These sways combined with the good feeling we had associated with eating the candy all added to the cumulative sway.

Overtime, the sways can go from external factors to internal choices, a process called *internalizing*. Once internalized, the sways can eventually become our unthinking preferences, even our habits that make us uncomfortable if we don't do them. We prefer the comfort of choosing the same, familiar thing, even when choosing bad stuff.[6] With so many choices to make in life, it's nice sometimes to not think and stick with what we know. Sways can even get us into a contrarian habit of always *not* choosing something, such as always avoiding the choice others take. Ironically, those who do so think themselves independent, but often, they don't realize their choice is still a sway, dependent on and needing to wait for others to choose first. (See lesson 5.4.)

There's nothing wrong with sticking to your familiar choice, of course, as long as you are smart about it. Sometimes, the old choice has a history of being a good one. Sometimes, however, the new or different choice is better and maybe even more productive and efficient or exciting and adventurous.

Sways are powerful forces in choosing for two reasons. First, they are subtle and happen over such a long period, we hardly notice them or how they affect us over time. (See lesson 5.5.)

Second, sways make life easier and so we welcome them. Remember how we said in the last chapter that hardly anyone likes to work more than they have to? It would be tedious to have to consciously weigh out every choice possibility every time when you have made the same choice dozens of times before. In fact, part of being smart is learning lessons that you apply to future circumstances. So something as simple as buying food shouldn't be complicated. If you already have a preference, why fret about it?

The cautionary response is that sometimes, it may be a bad choice, or at least not right for you. Even if we are looking at all the factors that influence your choice inside and outside of you, rational and nonrational, it always should remain *your* choice. Choices are best made by the individual for him- or herself, not in response to a historical chorus of people who may not even know him or her.

A sway can also look like it's the natural order of the universe or a coincidence, with things seemingly popping up out of nowhere to remind you of something you liked in the past. You see the snack you loved years ago in the store. Sometimes, however, the coincidental reference back has been cleverly orchestrated by a marketing "man behind the curtain" disguising his sway on your choice.[7] Just look at scoreboards at a game.

Sways are especially potent on young choosers because the younger a consumer is, the more they can be swayed, like a young tree that bends more to the wind. They don't have the experience—one could say the strong roots and trunk—to resist messaging. They are also eager to please and copy adults, called *aspirational motivation*. (See lesson 5.6.)

In 1992 marketing professor James McNeal wrote a book, *Kids as Customers*,[8] that said that advertising and marketing to kids was like selling to them in three different ways.[9] First, kids have their own money from their allowance and jobs. Most of a kid's money is disposable, meaning they have few necessities or obligations, such as rent or bills to pay. Second, kids influence their parents in what their parents consider buying.[10] Third, constantly messaging kids can create lifelong customers that stick with a brand, as we said before, out of familiarity or habit.[11] Gotta start those stalagmites early! (See lesson 5.7.)

It's one thing if someone, such as a peer, tries to convince you to make a choice but then lets you choose. It's another when they are using secret tricks and methods to tilt what's supposed to be *your* choice to achieve what's really best for them. One might call that manipulation. It's even worse when the trickster is a seasoned adult and the ones being tricked are innocent kids. It's like a professional team playing in a peewee league. (See lesson 5.8.)

So what should we do when we come to a choice, such as whether to choose the popular path or the road less traveled, and we already feel inclined or swayed to take one or the other? The trick is to ask *why* we are starting with a preference, and is that the better choice here and now? Are things different now so that it's time to change? Are *we* different enough to consider change? Is the potential of a greater reward worth the risk? We might feel drawn to a choice because it's the cool or popular choice, and we always want to be cool or popular, but we have to ask if the popular choice is right for us. Of course, it can be OK to still go with the cool or popular choice; people look at restaurant reviews for a reason. (See lesson 5.9.)

On the other hand, if we let the swayers make our choices for us, especially major ones, we become like the tree blown by the wind or, even worse, like a leaf that has no fixed place of its own but just goes where the wind takes it. If we, as consumers, become captured by one brand or messenger, then they don't have to worry about making their product the best quality or the lowest price. They know we will just be swayed and do what they say. The capturing of a consumer, by the way, applies as much to those pushing a political message, value, or point of view as it does to a consumer good. (See lesson 5.10.)

We've been talking about outsiders swaying our choices, even trapping us, by using sways to capture our choice selection. Weirdly, we can also capture ourselves by *self-swaying*.

As we've said, it's hard to make so many choices each time and think about everything. We have plenty of other stuff on our mind to have to add weighing out the pros and cons of every choice. So humans have a little trick of using mental shortcuts, which are sometimes fancily referred to by people who study decision-making as *heuristics*.

You go to get ice cream with a friend, and there are so many flavors to choose from. Your friend knows what she wants, chock-o-cricks.[12] You are asked what you want, but you are not sure. The people in line behind you seem impatient; everyone's staring. You feel the pressure as the clerk glares. What do you do? You quickly reason that your friend and you agree on many things, like clothes and music, so maybe you would also agree on ice cream flavor. "Make it two!" you say.

These little rules or shortcuts we develop can be helpful and save time and mental effort, like thinking that if a restaurant is popular, it must be good, or you always taking the road less traveled. We couldn't live without them. The problem comes when the rule becomes a nonthinking habit that we live by without asking if the mental shortcut should always apply. The restaurant might be overcharging because it is so popular—and you can get better food elsewhere. The road less traveled might be that way because of snakes. If we always choose just based on our shortcuts, we can trap ourselves by our own self-sway! (See lesson 5.11.)

Going with swaying winds is not always bad, especially if the wind is at your back. One such sway that can push us along is our opting for doing things that are fun. Educators call it *gamification*, but it's the simple idea that tasks are not as bad to do if an element of challenge or fun is added. Can I rake the leaves faster than I did it yesterday or faster than how long my sibling took—and still do a good job? It can make a task a little less tiresome or boring. Gamers familiar with role-playing games (RPGs) and their quest-like structure have mentally endured boring situations in the real world by turning it in their mind into a quest-like adventure with partitioned tasks to accomplish, with the most difficult parts being boss monsters. Oppositional competition can make one more aware of people trying to take advantage of them in marketing and messaging, like a detective game. Asking who is telling the truth as well as thinking about motives can make a person a better consumer of messages. Of course, a great part of gaming is earning the rewards, so building in levels and tiers of rewards as one accomplishes more can get one across the finish line.[13]

Again, there are a lot of different facets to sway. In sum, being swayed is so much a part of life, especially for a kid constantly being told what they "should" do, one stops feeling it after a while. It's like walking in the wind or wading in the ocean with gently pushing waves. You don't realize you are off course or not where you thought till you look up and consciously realize you are not where you thought you were. You've been moved without knowing it. The key, then, is to be aware of sways. That way you can choose for yourself whether to go with the sway or resist it. (See lesson 5.12.)

NOTES

1. Robert Frost, "The Road Not Taken," Poetry Foundation, accessed , https://www.poetryfoundation.org/poems/44272/the-road-not-taken.

2. WegENT, "Survey: Do NFL Fans Stay Loyal to Their Teams after Moving?," *Wegryn Enterprises* (blog), October 12, 2021, https://wegrynenterprises.com/2021/10/12/survey-do-nfl-fans-stay-loyal-to-their-teams-after-moving/. Most people root for their hometown team or the one they grew up with. In one survey of NFL fans, half said they would travel back to their hometown to watch their home team play. Playing off of this hometown preference, comedian Jerry Seinfeld notes that we love a player while he plays for our home team but no longer root for him when he goes to another team. Seinfeld concludes that what we are really therefore cheering for is the uniform or laundry. We want our hometown laundry to beat the laundry of the rival town.

3. See, for example, Ori Brafman and Rom Brafman, *Sway: The Irresistible Pull of Irrational Behavior* (New York: Doubleday, 2009).

4. Most people know that sunlight affects the direction of plant growth, but wind can also affect how and in what direction plants grow.

5. This is made up. But who knows? We may be on to something new here.

6. Hence we have the expression "The devil you know is better than the devil you don't."

7. Such as our re-referencing of *The Wizard of Oz* here. See the preface to this book.

8. James U. McNeal, *Kids as Customers: A Handbook of Marketing to Children* (New York: Lexington Books, 1992).

9. McNeal did not use the term *nudge*, as it had not been popularized yet as a behavioral economics term.

10. Kids influencing parents was delightfully called by others the *nag factor*.

11. See, J. Manjusha, S. Mitra, and L. Bhooshetty, "Is Nostalgia Marketing a Game-Changer for Toy Industry?" *Ilkogretim Online* 20, no. 5 (2021): 1820–31, https://doi.org/10.17051/ilkonline.2021.05.200. Such inculcation of a positive sentiment can even then be passed on to the next generation as older consumers buying for younger ones are motivated by a sense of nostalgia.

12. You didn't know it came as an ice cream flavor too?

13. Some teachers (even those who write books on behavioral economics) use gamifying tricks on themselves, such as placing a stack of papers to be graded on top of a keyboard. Once the papers are graded, the teacher has dug down to the "treasure" and can now play a computer game.

Chapter 5 Accompanying Lessons

LESSON 5.1. REBEL REBEL

Focus of Exploration

Rebellion as a sway, *group pressure*.

Intro Questions / Thoughts for Students

Do you consider yourself more of a rebel, going against popular opinion, or a conformist, going with popular opinion? When are you more one and when more the other?

Do you like to be different from the crowd at times? When? Do you ever intentionally try to be different? Do you ever let your self-perception as a conformist or rebel guide you in choosing?

Activity

Think of different preferences you have: your favorite food, style of dress, activities, and/or sports teams you support. For each, think about whether you tend to have the same preference as groups you are with when choosing that, or do you tend to be different from the rest? If you can, try to think of how you came to have that preference. Was it because of what the group wanted? You can make two lists of your preferences, one where you comport (agree) with the group and one where you disagree or go against the group preference.

Follow-Up Questions/Discussions

What patterns do you see in your preferences? When are you more likely to be different or comport? Is it determined more by the type of choice or the group you are with?

The group is a powerful influence, as it is a social power exerted on you over time. The "group" can even be one person in authority, such as a teacher telling you what to do. Can you add some cases where you generally comport or do differently than what one person in power tells you to do?

Group pressure, also known as *crowding* or, in some cases, *peer pressure*, is a powerful force, as a person can't help but be influenced in their choices by people around them and their choices. You have probably felt it. Imagine, then, being around people who make the same choices over time. It might create an impression that their group choice was always the best—or even the only—choice to make. Are there any choices you make that you really never consciously made? You just chose it because it seemed *the* choice everyone made? For such a choice, are there other options?

Sometimes, the pressure to go with or against the group is actually coming from inside us. The chooser wants respect or to not be embarrassed or judged badly by the group. Does that happen to you? How many of your choices above are more because of your feelings about how the group might react to your choice (or how you *think* they will react)? Often, people worry about how they will be judged by others only to find out others didn't judge them at all. It was 100 percent in the person's mind!

Sometimes, we differ from the group's choice simply because we want something else. It is no judgment on the group's choice. Sometimes we differ because we *want* to be different from the group, to rebel. Why do people want to rebel at times? Does it feel good to intentionally stand apart sometimes? Why?

Rebelling because you think of yourself as a rebel is a sway, as you are bringing into the present choice a predetermined opinion of yourself. If you have a reputation for doing things a certain way and your choice is based on you wanting to keep that reputation, that's also a sway. When is it OK to choose to maintain an image, and when is it better to think about redefining your image?

What happens if everyone is a rebel? When is it better, even cooler, to conform or go with the group? Are there people that count on you at times to conform and not rebel? How can we know when it is better to choose to conform and when is it better to rebel? When is it more important to choose what's best for the group rather than for ourselves?

How does rebellion look online? Does it look the same as IRL? Does it work the same way? Do you need the group present and watching to rebel against them? Does rebellion need to be seen, such as in a comment that disagrees? Can just not participating be a rebellion?

LESSON 5.2. "I DON'T THINK WE'RE IN KANSAS ANYMORE"

Focus of Exploration

Passive sways, such as location.

Intro Questions / Thoughts for Students

What preferences or choices do you have that are based on where you live? Do you root for the local sports team? Is there a custom or festival in your town that you like going to or participating in? Is there a food your area is known for that you like? How might all of these be different if you had lived somewhere else?

Activity

Interview parents, teachers, and other adults about where they grew up. It's better to find adults who grew up in a different place than where they live now or even people who lived in several places as they grew up.

- What were their favorite things growing up that related to where they lived—a favorite food, activity, or team? Is there anything else, such as a favorite season of the year?
- As they moved, how did their choices and preferences change because of location?
- What choices do they make or preferences do they now have that still come from where they grew up? Do they think they will change?

You can present your findings in a chart, listing locations and then listing favorite foods, activities, interests, and so forth.

Follow-Up Questions/Discussions

Do the people you interviewed remember choices that were based on location? Were the choices more of one category, such as food or activities? Why do you think that is?

Do people make a lot of choices now that are based on where they grew up years ago? Does that mean their present choice was at least partially determined by what happened long ago? How far back can sways still affect our choices now?

You were asked to interview adults because their many years offer a longer perspective. You can see how things that happened long ago still sway their choices now. What about you? Are there things about where or how you grew up years ago that sway your choices today? What about friends in a different part of town or neighborhood?

Sways don't have to be planned. They can just happen, especially if they repeat over a long time. If you find people who grew up in the same far-away place but for much different periods, see if there is a different impact of the location on their choices.

LESSON 5.3. BLOWIN' IN THE WIND

Focus of Exploration

Sway, drawing inferences, *correlations*.

Intro Questions / Thoughts for Students

What are some things that you can't see; hear; or, in some other way, can't fully sense, but you know they are there? How do you know?

Is there anything you can figure out—deduce—from the effect, or change, that you see? For example, if you look outside and see a tree moving or that the ground is wet, can you make a deduction that it might be windy or rainy? What else?

Detectives deduce choices and things that happened in the past by what they see now. For example, if they see a fingerprint, they deduce that someone touched that object. If you closed your bedroom door and then later saw it open, what can you deduce happened? How sure can you be? What are the many possibilities, and how likely is each to have happened?

Activity

You are going to play a detective in the world.

- Look for things you can't see, hear, or otherwise sense but you know are there by how others react to them. Maybe you see people cover their ears, like they hear a harsh sound you don't, or they scratch themselves and you don't see what's causing the itch.
- Look for things where you can guess about another person's choice without having seen them make that choice. You could be at a restaurant and see a table that has not been cleaned yet. Can you tell how many people sat there and what they ate? Remember not to touch it, though. It may not be clean, and you might be disturbing a "crime scene!"

Follow-Up Questions/Discussions

What you are doing is using facts and observations to draw *inferences*—initial conclusions based on the information you have. They're not the same as the facts themselves because you are adding logic and reasoning. Inferences are drawn by using a combination of induction, looking at details (e.g., number of plates at a table) to conclude what the big picture was (how many people ate there), and using deduction, applying big-picture rules of life (restaurants don't randomly lay food on tables) to make conclusions like "There is a half-eaten burger on the table, so someone must have ordered it." The great fictional detective Sherlock Holmes used both!

Drawing inferences is tricky because there is usually more than one explanation. If you see a person on the ground, they may have tripped, been pushed, or just laid down for a moment. Their behavior on the ground can be a clue to what happened before. A good detective must think about which explanation is more likely. What are other explanations for the things you observed? How much can you rule them out?

Once you draw an inference, your job as a social scientist is not done. You can look for further evidence that supports, or *corroborates*, the inference. They might change a variable to see if it makes a difference (like going to another restaurant). Most of all, a social scientist must be open to changing it if new information says they should.

There are potential dangers to making wrong inferences. For example, one might see that when people eat more ice cream, they get more sunburns; therefore, ice cream causes sunburn. Actually, both things—people eating ice cream and getting sunburned—are more likely in summer when it is hot. Can you think of other things that have a relationship of happening together or are connected, creating a *correlation*, but one is not the cause of the other? Also, sometimes things that appear connected can be just a plain old, boring coincidence.

How does all this about the idea of invisible or unseen things affecting others relate to making a choice and being swayed? Could a bad experience or past memory sway what you choose now? What about your mood? If you have a really good or bad day and then you come to a choice, like what to have for dinner, do you think that can make a difference? Ask your parents what comfort food is! Have you ever had a friend react strangely, such as getting very angry, when given a choice, and you found out later that something had happened before that had put them in that frame of mind?

LESSON 5.4. HOW LONG HAS THIS BEEN GOIN' ON?

Focus of Exploration

Habitual sways, sways becoming nonthinking habits rather than choices.

Intro Questions / Thoughts for Students

Is there anything you always do? They can be choices about what you wear or do. They can be tied to a day, such as always doing an activity on a certain day of the week. They can also be habits or customs, like always patting your pet before you leave the house.

What are some things a group you belong to—family, friends, or your class—always do? It can be a method or procedure or a group choice. Maybe it is a pizza-and-movie night or the classic "On Wednesdays we wear pink!"

Activity

Think of choices you make either personally or as part of a group where you don't think about the choice, you just do it. Try now to reflect on those nonthinking choices, like if you were a reporter interviewing yourself:

- What is the choice you have been making without thinking?
- How long have you been making that choice?
- How did you first come to make that choice?
- Why do you keep making that choice? Are you the right person to be judging if it is a good choice or the best choice?
- Can the choice be improved or even changed?

Write up your interview like a news story interview. Look at some interviews online for a model.

Follow-Up Questions/Discussions

Can you recall about when each activity stopped being an active, present choice and became something you don't think about but just do? Why is that hard to do?

What are the advantages to not having to rechoose and just doing something as it has been done? Are there any disadvantages? How often should a habit of past choices be reexamined? For groups, how is it best discussed? Is there crowd pressure to not change?

If your choice goes back a long way, are you the same version of you as back when the choice was first made or became a sway? How are you different? Does the choice still fit the new, present you?

LESSON 5.5. I AM

Focus of Exploration

Self-perception and self-identity as affecting choice.

Intro Questions / Thoughts for Students

Do you ever make a choice based on how you see yourself? How about how you want to see yourself? For example, if I see myself as a cat lover, I will look to buy birthday cards and other things with cats on them, but not dogs. Is that OK?

In what ways are you the same person as you were five years ago, and in what ways are you a new or different person?

Activity

Make a list that fills in the phrase *I am a ____ person*.
Include the following in your list:

- A product you love to buy/use
- Your favorite activity
- Your favorite or best subject in school
- Something about your character (honest, caring, or mischievous)
- Anything else that you or people who know you well would use to describe you, such as talkative or laughing or fashion smart

For each of these, think about how seeing yourself this way influences your choices. Can you think of a time for each when you made a choice in part or totally to fit how you see yourself? Can you think of a time your choice did not fit with how you see yourself?

Follow-Up Questions/Discussions

Was this easier to do for some categories than others? Why was that? Does it depend on how much you think that category or response describes you?

What kind of person do you hope to be in five years? Are there any changes to the list? How might that be reflected in your choices in the next five years?

Did you ever make choices that you felt were the opposite or very different from who you are? How did it feel to make those choices? Did you learn anything about yourself from that experience?

Some people say your choices and actions reflect who you already are. Others say your choices and actions make you who you are. What is the difference? Which view gives you more power to choose or change who you are? Which view do you like better?

LESSON 5.6. YOUR CHOICE, BUT IT SHOULD BE . . .

Focus of Exploration

Aspirational motivation and *sways*.

Intro Questions / Thoughts for Students

Do you have any plans right now about what you want to do or be for a career as an adult? Where did you get that idea? Have you ever seen a depiction of your plans in media?

Besides a career, what other aspects do you imagine for your adult life or hope it will include? Will you be in a relationship and, if so, with what kind of person? Do you have a particular place or kind of place—beach, city, small town, or mountains—that you hope to live in?

One of the great things about adulthood is the ability to determine and define one's own identity, or how you see yourself and present yourself to others. Are there any parts of your adult identity, such as your gender, ethnicity, or personality, that you have an idea of what they will be or hope they will be?

Activity

Write out both your professional and personal aspirations for your adult self. For both of these groups, look at media for depictions of these aspects. Don't look up specifically, "What is it like to be a(n) [insert aspiration]?" but try to just take note when you see a depiction, like a character in a show, of some part of what you envision your adult life to be. Take note if the depiction shows the following:

- How they achieved or created that part of their life (or whether they just grew to be that)
- The day-in, day-out, regular aspect of that part or just when it is exciting or dramatic
- The challenges needed to get the good parts out of it
- How that part fits or meshes with other aspects of their identity or life
- Any doubts or issues the character has with that part of their life, and how those doubts or issues are resolved

Follow-Up Questions/Discussions

Of course, what you are seeing is more for entertainment than a documentary for information. Still, do you think people form general ideas of what being that type of adult is like based on all the messaging? The show makers will say they can't show all aspects of something, which is true, but if they all show only the exciting or dramatic parts, is that a problem?

Do you think all the depictions of some aspect of adulthood, whether of a career or of something personal like relationships, can sway people to think about that aspect in a certain way over time? What can you do to get a more accurate idea of what it's like to be something you wish to be as an adult? A good check is to ask adults who are living as adults in one of the ways you wish to be if media portrayals are accurate.

Sometimes, media will lightly touch on an issue but not go too deep because of time or the plot wants to go elsewhere. A character might say, "It's hard to be the only woman jet fighter," and nothing more. Are there any aspects of your life, especially as to your identity, where you see a possibility for conflict with other aspects? Can you seek out adults who are navigating those issues already and ask them?

LESSON 5.7. THREE OF ME

Focus of Exploration

James McNeal's three-part model of kids as consumers, *internalizing* choices.

Intro Questions / Thoughts for Students

How are family choices made in your family? Is there a vote? Do certain family members have the final or only say? Does it depend on what is being chosen? How so?

Even if you don't make the choice, in what ways do you influence family choices?

Activity

Choose a family activity or something you do regularly. It can be a meal, movies, family-night games, or a family trip. Whatever you choose, write out for it the following questions:

- What choices do you get to make?
- What choices do you try to nudge your parents to make?
- What are your parents' or family's choices that you like and want to keep doing when you have your own family?

If you can, try to do this for several family activities. Then discuss it with your family.

Follow-Up Questions/Discussions

How did your influence or say on choices vary by the kind of family activity?

Have there been any choices you'd made that then became the family choice over time? That is your nudge becoming a sway for your parents. Are you getting more choices over time?

For your parents' choices that you influence, do you use more open, overt nudges ("I want you to choose") or indirect, subtle nudges ("It would be nice to have")? Which works better? Do you think your parents and other family members always know when you are trying to nudge them?

Do you ever see others try to nudge your parents, such as an ad that shows how happy the kids are that the parents made a specific choice? Point it out to your parents.

The hardest messages to see are when the messengers want you to keep doing the activity you already do but for the rest of your life. They want their nudging message to become *internalized* so that it is a sway for the rest of your life ("I have always liked"). Is it possible to see how they do that in any one message? Ask your parents what they have done or chosen since they were young and why they have done it for so long.

If you don't like the influence you have in family choices, how can you express that? Can you have a family meeting? Can you come up with a proposed change in your choice power? What are you willing to give up for it, or what responsibilities are you willing to take on for the increased power of more choice or more say in choices?

How are choices about the internet and social apps made in your family? In what ways do you get to choose? In what ways do your parents choose what you do online? What choices about social apps and being online do you think you will and will not make when you are an adult? If you have an older sibling, ask them how their online choices have changed over time.

LESSON 5.8. INDEPENDENCE OR INTERDEPENDENCE?

Focus of Exploration

Disguised corporate nudging, pretended rebellion against culture.

Intro Questions / Thoughts for Students

People like rebels, or the people who speak their mind against the established brands and ways of thinking—called "the establishment." Who are some of your favorite rebel brands or personalities?

If you found out that a rebel brand was made by or paid by the establishment, such as an independent cola brand that was made by a large, century-old brand, would that affect your opinion of the independent brand? What if you found out that your favorite rebel personality or influencer was paid to look rebellious? Would that change your opinion of them?

Activity

Look for "rebel" brands that promote themselves as fighting against the establishment or for the little guy, those outside of big power. Look into who owns them or how established they are. Are they in fact a little guy or a sub-brand of a big company?

For a personality you like, such as an influencer, look up who their *sponsors* are, or who pays them. Do they have ties or promotional deals with anyone that might influence their message?

Follow-Up Questions/Discussions

If you found out the rebel or influencer was not so much a rebel away from cameras, would that change how you feel about them? What if you found out the humble, plainclothes personality lived in a penthouse with fancy clothes and that the regular-guy rebel was a *persona*?

If there is a positive message, does it matter what the company actually does? For example, if a company sends a message to empower women and girls, but the company itself does not hire more women or even treats them poorly in some parts of its company, how much does that affect your response to their positive messaging?

You might think that a company would not like it when a personality says bad things about it, but there is also the saying "There is no such thing as bad publicity." The idea is that as long as people are talking about the brand in some way, it is good for the company. How do you feel about that? Is it the same for you personally, that you would rather have people talk about you, even say some mildly negative things, than not talk about you at all?

Have you ever seen two brands or personalities at war with each other? How can a feud actually help each side? Can it affect customer loyalty and identity, swaying them over a long time to attach and identify with one or the other? Do you think that's ever intentional?

Why would members of the establishment send a message to rebel? Is there a benefit to their *posing*? Have you ever seen people you know pretend to be rebels?

LESSON 5.9. GO WITH THE SWAY

Focus of Exploration

Sways turning into habits, interview skills.

Intro Questions / Thoughts for Students

Have you ever had a friend tell you they always do something, or you saw it was their custom to do something? How was it to watch them do it? Did you just accept it? Did you try it? Did you think it was the right thing to do?

Has a friend ever tried to get you to choose something because they had always made that choice? How did you feel?

Activity

Interview a friend about a choice they have made the same way for a long time. It can be a food, style of clothing, or an activity. Ask them when they first started doing it and why. What were the reasons they started? Are their reasons for doing it at the beginning as good today as back then? Also, ask how much of their continuing the choice today is because they think about it and agree with the reasons, and ask how much is just habit.

Importantly, ask your friend if he or she thinks his or her choice is right for you. Why or why not?

Follow-Up Questions/Discussions

We did a previous exercise where you looked at your own longtime choices (see lesson D, above). Now you are examining those of a friend. What is the difference between looking at your own and those of a friend? Which is harder to do? Why? What can you learn from examining the sways of another person?

One advantage of interviewing a friend is that you can compare their *subjective* view ("I never wear pink") with your firsthand, observed, *objective* view (you have seen them wear pink several times). Are there advantages to interviewing or examining the sways of a third person who isn't your friend, even someone very different from you?

As your friend talked about their sway, did you think about your own sways? Why is that? Does thinking about your own sways while listening to someone else help or detract from your investigation?

If you are uncomfortable with your friend's choices that have become sways, what is the best thing to do? Is there a difference between you thinking they are not right for you and them being not right for your friend? When do you think you have a duty to speak out or even tell someone else if the choice your friend keeps making is dangerous?

Often, when someone has a sway, they try to convince others to start making the same choice in their life. Why do you think people do this? Do they think it's good for everyone? Do they feel better about a choice if others also choose it? Have you ever tried to convince others to choose the same thing to feel better about choosing it yourself?

Look for comments online where people say "everyone" should do something or that, if you don't, you are a loser. Which is more impactful to you, the voice of a friend telling you to start making a choice or thousands of people online telling you to make the choice? Why?

There is an art to interviewing that takes practice. You want to give just enough focus to a topic in the question, but then let the person have plenty of space to give their opinion with you pointing them toward a certain answer. One tool is the interviewer giving a slight smile, nod, and then their silence after a response. It often encourages the respondent to add more on their own. Try it!

LESSON 5.10. MY OWN OPINION IS TO AGREE WITH YOURS

Focus of Exploration

Sway in ideas, *anchoring*.

Intro Questions / Thoughts for Students

Is there anyone whose opinion or view of the world you nearly always believe? Are there different people for different topics where you trust them to almost always be right?

Is there anyone or any source that you think if they say something, it must be true? What about the opposite? Is there a person or source that you think if they say something, it must *not* be true?

Activity

Make a list of people or sources—like sites online—where you believe almost everything they tell you without you feeling a need to double-check. Break it down by topic, such as sports, fashion, relationships, and so forth, and list a person or source for each. For each listed, list *why* you have put such trust in them. What have they done to be unquestionable?

Now list people or sources you won't believe. Again, list out topics if it helps, and list people by each. Indicate why you won't believe them.

Follow-Up Questions/Discussions

For the people and places you trust, is it because you have researched their accuracy or background or have double-checked them, and they have always been right? How many do you believe because other people say they do or tell you to believe them? If it's more because of other people, then is your faith in that source or in the people who told you? Are they 100 percent trustworthy? Could they be biased in their opinion? The same questions apply to the people or sources you don't trust.

When we choose to 100 percent believe or not believe a source without double-checking, or we do so because other people tell us to do that, we are letting others think for us, creating a sway on our choices of what to believe in. For which topics is it OK to let others sway you in your thinking, and for which should you hold on to the power and choose for yourself?

If you can, choose a source you absolutely trust in and one you do not. Choose a topic and look deeply into what each says. How much do they have in common? If they do have things in common, what does that tell you about your 100 percent trust / don't-trust belief? If they differ, do they differ as to the facts or their opinion? Why is that distinction important? Is there a third source you can check?

When one starts with a belief and then measures everything relative to that first belief, it is called *anchoring*. Once anchored, even truthful or reasonable counterinformation seems wrong. If you think your house is worth millions of dollars, you might see a reasonable offer as too low and refuse it. In the same way, if we start with an anchored belief that someone or something is good or bad, and we see solid evidence to the contrary, we doubt the evidence and do not reevaluate our beliefs. Have you experienced that or seen it in somebody? How can you guard against anchoring your beliefs in one source of information or one person's opinion?

LESSON 5.11. SHORTCUT OR CUT SHORT?

Focus of Exploration

Heuristics.

Intro Questions / Thoughts for Students

Have you ever faced a complicated choice and then decided by using a simple rule to cut through it all, like "If it smells bad, don't eat it" or "Never believe what they say"?

Activity

Make a list of all the rules of thumb that you use to help make complicated choices and situations easier. What are the ones that tell you to always choose a certain option? What are ones that tell you *not* to do something? Does your family or your group of friends have a dos and don'ts list of rules for choosing?

For each rule think about them as a sway in your choosing. How did the rule come about? Is the rule still valid? When and how should it be evolved for who you are and circumstances today? Do you need whole new rules?

Follow-Up Questions/Discussions

When you were younger, adults tried to keep rules simple. They made the shortcuts absolute, like "Don't talk to strangers." Now that you are older, you can start to see that life is complicated. "Not always" starts to be a possibility. Young campers may learn to think of red berries like a stop sign—"Don't eat them!" Of course, strawberries are red and OK to eat, so if you were starving, you would miss out. In what areas have you seen the most not-always rules creeping into your heuristic shortcuts (rules of thumb)?

Some people prefer to choose by absolute rules, like a paint-by-numbers art. Others like more of an open, blank canvas they can fill in how they choose. Which is more you and in what areas?

Around middle school, right and wrong seem to go from black and white to often being gray. Who do you go to for help in figuring out the gray areas and how to change your personal rules to meet the new complications of life? Does the person you go to depend on which topic?

LESSON 5.12. CAN THE WIND BLOW ONLINE?

Focus of Exploration

Sways and *heuristics* online.

Intro Questions / Thoughts for Students

You live in two worlds, online and IRL. In many ways they are the same in that you make choices and then feel the result of those choices and adjust. They are also different. Off the top of your head, how are the two worlds different in terms of consequences?

What are big choices you make IRL that you don't make online? What are big choices you make online that you don't make IRL? What are similar choices you make in both worlds? Are there different factors that affect your choices?

Activity

Think of choices that you often make both online and IRL, such as with shopping, what to say to a friend who is sad, whether to share a bit of gossip, or what to do when you hear or read something that makes you uncomfortable. Make a Venn diagram to show which choices are in each world and which are shared in both. For each choice, think of what is your rule of thumb or general first thought about such choices, called a *heuristic*, that generally sways your choice or reaction. You can put a number by each choice in your diagram and then list the numbers below with each heuristic you use by the number corresponding to the choice. For choices in both worlds, does the heuristic for one world work in the other? If not, or if you modify it, list both by the number note.

Follow-Up Questions/Discussions

As we said before, heuristics can give us a starting point, but we need some flexibility. Which seems to need more rule flexibility to you, online or IRL?

Are there situations or choices online that you just don't have IRL? For those can you make up a new heuristic to sway your choices?

Heuristics IRL, like "Don't eat red berries in the wild" come from smart people who came before us. If you are coming up with heuristics for being online, it also makes sense to ask smart people who have experience online, like scouts who would check out the path up ahead. Ask your parents or older siblings what advice or shortcuts they would recommend for being online.

A big part of heuristics is that the rules work because you are the same person who will act in the same way whenever the situation arises. Do you think you act the same online and IRL, such as being nice to friends? Are you the same person in terms of the choices you make? If you don't feel like you act the same, what is the difference? Why do you think you act differently? Do the different versions of you need different heuristics?

Putting numbers and then adding explanations is called notation. Generally, people use notes like this to either cite the source for the information or to add an explanation or further information, which is what you are doing here. Look through a nonfiction book, like a textbook, at its citations. Which do you see more of, citation or explanatory notes? Why do authors use them?

Chapter Six

The Tween Mind

Algebra, introduced to most students in their early tween years, is a big cognitive leap. It's going from doing math with numbers having distinct and certain values to solving equations with letters that represent unknown, indistinct, and possibly varying values. It's the introduction of abstraction, or in nonmath words, the *maybe*s and *not always* into formerly "What is?" equations. Thinking abstractly is a skill that requires both biological developmental readiness and the experience to master the art. That's two variables, and each variable differs for each individual.[1]

If an algebra single-variable equation can be challenging for some eighth graders, imagine asking fifth or sixth graders to do it, let alone multivariables on the level of calculus.

Unfortunately, we do. It's called *social calculus*, and youth begin to face such equations going from elementary to middle school. It might not be strictly mathematical, but in many ways, it's more abstract and more difficult.

What is the limit to how much you can tease or push back against someone until it is too far, considering both your behavior and the other person's feelings? How much should you go along with a crowd to fit in, doing things you don't particularly want to do? How much does that person really like—or "like likes"—you? Numbers don't lie, but people do or, at the very least, are of unknown values.

We have Jim Hawkins,[2] Huck Finn, Billy Batson,[3] Meg Murry,[4] Peter Parker,[5] and Harry Potter—over a hundred years of fictional characters, all in their preteens or early teens. They all are challenged to face a confusing, abstract adult world that requires immediate deftness in social calculus just to survive. Often, they discover they have strange new powers or skills, which they must harness and control as they are thrown from the relative safety of childhood into the adult world of chaos and danger. The heroes often realize that what they thought they knew about the world was incomplete or wrong. They must learn about the real world even as they simultaneously try to figure out who they are themselves.

Why is the formula timelessly appealing? Because, in a nutshell, it's what being a *tween* or early teen is all about.

Tween is a vague term that seems to be at its root a short form of "between," as in the age between being a child and being a teenager. It's characteristically a chaotic time of emotional, hormonal growth coupled with the onset of abstract thought. Age wise, we will use the term to define roughly the ages of ten to twelve, although the age any individual enters or leaves tweendom varies by biological development and environment. (See lesson 6.1.)

The transition into middle school, coinciding with the tween years, is when kids begin to realize the world is not as neat or as simple as they thought in elementary years. People aren't either good guys or bad guys; almost everyone is a mix. Rules of life such as "Don't lie" start to come with an asterisk that says sometimes it may be better to shade or even omit the truth, such as when sparing someone's feelings. The previously straight and narrow path suddenly opens up to show many available twisty-turny trails. The expectation is for the tween to start exploring the paths they want to take, even if they don't know where each path leads. It's the beginning of consequential choice making, often with no do-overs.

While the tween is confronted with a whole new view of the world, he or she also starts becoming a radically changed person as well. Like the heros with strange new superpowers that they don't fully have command of yet, puberty starts taking hold of the young person's body. While we most clearly see the effects on the outside of a tween's body, the biggest change is going on inside.[6]

As hormones step into the driver's seat of the tween's human body, a tiny, almond-shaped sliver in the brain called the *amygdala* goes through an explosive change worthy of any superhero origin story. The amygdala is generally the source of emotional response, and it comes to near-adult powers with puberty. By contrast, the *prefrontal cortex*,[7] the seat of executive function that balances reason and emotion-based thought and is the checker of impulsiveness, does not fully mature until around age twenty-five.[8]

What this means is that for the first fifteen or so years after entering their tweens, young people are learning how to make choices with the emotional amygdala screaming and while the prefrontal cortex is still finding its voice.[9] Tweens may overlaugh, overcry, overworry, and overobsess even as they face their first unguided choices, not only about what they want to do but also who they want to be.[10] It's like a new driver who at first only knows to floor the gas pedal or slam on the brakes.

TWEEN MOTIVATORS

Before we go into how tweens specifically make choices, we need to first explore how tweens receive and process all the new data coming to them that they, in turn, use to then make their choices. Jean Piaget delineated stages of cognitive development that have remained the standard over eighty years after he first began his studies.[11] Two of his stages involve the tween years.

Dominating the tween years is the concrete operational stage. Here youth become aware of events and perspectives outside of themselves. They realize that others may have different experiences and feelings, though the child's understanding is limited by their still concrete thinking. The ability for abstract thought has not yet developed or is very primitive and unrefined. Youth in this stage are mini-anthropologists, wanting to take in as many observations as they can of the world and see if they can get a big picture from all the strange subjects they are observing.[12]

Piaget noted two tools that children use to sort the massive amount of data they collect, *classification* and *seriation*. Classification is sorting things into groups. A rose and a lily are different colors, but they can be grouped as flowers, while an apple is not. Seriation is to then arrange the things within classes by a logical order, such as by size or value. Both tools help the child both to understand the world and feel empowered to make choices. Many tweens exercise these skills by collecting and sorting things.

Consider how important cliques or social groups become in middle school. In elementary school almost everyone was a "friend" or, at most, was different but still part of the class. Tweens in middle school often start dividing up into jocks, social-focused kids, studiers, and so on. It's their way of making concrete the abstract reality and data dump that people are different and have different interests. It also allows unsure tweens to group and find an identity. Worse than having a bad reputation is having none at all and having to go it alone. Within groups, or as between groups themselves, a pecking order emerges, such as determining the "queen bee." This is seriation kicking in, as relative value is now assigned within classifications. (See lesson 6.2.)

Marketers have tapped into the tween valuation and choice-selection process for their own benefit. Classification and seriation have been used to nudge and, in the long term, develop sways in youth choice making. Tweens vie for who has the most and is the most knowledgeable about any given world's characters in games, online, or with other media forms. One can see the parallel extent of collect-them-all products marketed to tweens. Tweens put a coolness premium on being "in the know" about popular items. Product makers are all too happy to promise tweens such personal and social rewards if they will only buy their collections. Above all, marketers tell tweens that the worst thing in the world, far worse than spending money on things of little long-term interest or use, is to be the only one not doing it.[13] (See lesson 6.3.)

To understand the unfamiliar worlds they are stepping into, tweens are smart enough to watch and imitate more experienced people in it with *aspirational motivation*. As *newbies*, they still need guidance from adults, though they are also starting to see that what adults say and what adults do is not always the same. Tweens will watch what adults do and then look for a chance to show they can imitate and even outdo the adults to prove the tween is ready for such challenges.[14] (See lesson 6.4.)

In the process of figuring out the world, tweens are also figuring out about themselves as well. Tweendom is a time to try on many personalities and dispositions, including personalities and dispositions of the tween's choosing. They change frequently because, aside from the amygdala hijacking their mood every couple of minutes, the tween wants to change and try out different things.

TWEEN DRIVERS

Self-definition is a long-term goal. In the short term, tweens are looking for some immediately reinforcing feelings. Marketers to tweens identified four strong feelings, *drivers*, that tweens respond to:[15]

- *Fun*—Understanding the world is hard, and so tweens love any break in the seriousness and pressure. They especially like the fun of pointing out the inconsistency and ridiculousness of the supposedly logical grown-up world. It makes the world they are entering less scary. They love gotcha jokes and wordplay.[16]
- *Power*—While elementary children are still in their protected world, tweens find themselves at the bottom of the greater societal pyramid. They also feel the beginning surge of puberty power alluded to in the superhero and fantasy stories they love, and they are looking for outlets to use that power. Unfortunately, tweens often exert any such power against each other as an expression of seriation in the form of bullying. If a person is better at a game or social interaction, why, in the tween's mind, should he or she not flaunt it?
- *Freedom*—Tweens are still mostly tied to their family, but it doesn't mean they can't start to look to the possibility of independence. They want to try new things and would prefer not to have parental or older-sibling commentary on it. The hormone-infused emotional swings of the amygdala magnify their irritation at family constraints. Tweens begin to seek parental

advice less and often find it's preferable to not let the parents know what they are up to, inspired by both a desire for freedom and a fear of embarrassment. (See lesson 6.5.)

Belonging—Humans are tribal by nature. If a tween is starting to push away from parents, they need a new group for survival. They especially want one that understands their joys and challenges and sees them as an equal, not junior, participant. Membership in a tribe is tantamount to finding both an identity and a support group all in one. Tweens may not have the language skills to adequately express what they feel, so they appreciate peers who empathetically understand. The belonging drive hits a peak in the teen years, but that desire manifests early. (See lessons 6.6 and 6.7.)

In the end most tweens survive and even thrive in the turbulence of data gathering in the concrete operational stage. They then move into Piaget's formal operational stage sometime near the end of their tween or at the beginning of their teen years. This is when they obtain abstract thought and the developing skills to make hypotheses and think out consequences and plan pathways to goals. If the concrete operational stage of tween years is like being in a raft amid white-water rapids, going into the formal operational stage is like suddenly discovering a paddle with which to guide the raft. It will still take practice and experience to learn how to steer well—the fully developed prefrontal cortex is still about ten years away, but the surges of hormonal, mental, and physical power can start to be corralled, controlled, and harnessed in a direction the now teen desires. (See lesson 6.8.)

If all goes well, young people emerge on the other side of adolescence with the skills they need to make good choices as adults. Unfortunately, many tweens, while sailing through their first opportunities for independent choice making, crash against some nasty rocks. The hazards are potentially doubled, as tweens today not only make choices in the physical world but simultaneously make choices in the online world as well.

It may not be in the same numbers as Willy Wonka's factory, where four of the five invitees didn't make it to the end of the tour, because of their poor choices, but the magical, strange, inside world of virtual activity poses challenges disguised as sweets as well. There are at least five dangerous-choice situations in today's world of online tweens as relates to their cognitive development.

There is the *emotional outburst frozen in time*. Most adults can recount an incident from their own youth that they now regret, perhaps a rage against a parent or a regrettable outburst and tears against a friend. They are also glad that there were no recordings of it beyond a bad memory or an occasional embarrassing family story. Unfortunately, in today's world of the internet, such outbursts can be recorded and uploaded, or the tweens themselves can text their emotion-infused sentiments to the world in a mad instant.

And there it remains—forever. There really is no such thing as "delete" on the internet. Almost every app, platform, and website backs up its content regularly, and there are even programs designed so people can see how pages looked in the past.[17] Even if a poster acts quickly, the speed at which any post is seen, captured, and forwarded to others is hard to beat. Thus, in today's world, a momentary emotional outburst can have long-lasting dire consequences.[18] (See lesson 6.9.)

There is the *entrapping identity*. It's fun to try on new personalities or experiment with new likes and experiences; it's the joy of choice. Today a tween is a K-pop loving jock, but maybe next week, they want to try being a grunge, computer-nerd gamer, and then the week after that, they try a third type or a combination of the two.

Despite the initial visioning of the internet as a place for looking at things from different perspectives, even as a place to evolve one's choices, it has many ossified parts today. Many places on the web have become walled-off zones for "true" members only. People are encouraged to declare which team they are on. Fans of celebrities or music groups declare themselves a cohesive, forever-devoted army who must absolutely choose to support the icon no matter what.

Cohesive, supportive identity is fine. Some groups, however, come to demand single, unquestioning loyalty or, rather, sworn fealty in choices. Due to the isolating effect within single-interest or fan groups, *echo chambers* are created where messages and feelings get amplified as they keep getting repeated, often out of proportion. They see people outside the group, with different interests or preferences, as wrong or even a threat.

This is counter to what should be a tween's celebrated exploration of even alternative ideas and perspectives. Trying on different hats is what should be encouraged, especially for tweens first exploring the world's options; they should not be condemned for disloyalty. At the very least, tolerance should be maintained for those who are different, think different, or just plain have different tastes, such as in music. Ideally, tolerance should also be encouraged for those who are of different cultures, classes, upbringings, opinions, or identities. (See lesson 6.10.)

There is the *unreal victim*. An entrapping identity can restrict, even harm, the tween who wants to consider different perspectives. Monolithic-thinking groups can also nudge their members, especially tweens, to want to assert a group's superiority by way of thinking badly and even taking action against outsiders to the group. It's a superamplifier of the classification and seriation desires of tweens to the point of ill will and even harm.

Studies show that people who would not otherwise be prone to act maliciously or even violently can be incited to do so when in a crowd.[19] Unfortunately, the isolation that internet interest groups can create combined with the echo chamber effect can amplify antagonism toward those the group sees as outsiders. Because the antagonism is felt online at amorphous "thems," it becomes easy to lose sight of the other people's humanity. It's like throwing a rock at a crowd, forgetting that the crowd is made up of individuals who each can get very hurt by that rock. That's not to mention the collective effect of many rocks thrown at once. At the extremes, groups engage in *mobbing*, directing group animus toward the target by way of malicious texting or malicious pranking.[20]

We sometimes hear stories about clever mobs that fought back by tying up a perceived enemy's life or pulling a funny prank by ordering thousands of dollars of stuff in their name, but such acts have real costs to people's wallets,[21] reputations,[22] and even lives.[23] For a tween just exploring the nature of social interactions, being on the receiving end can be quite overwhelming. Based on a single rumor or prank, they might get tens, even hundreds, of texts that criticize them or threaten them. Even just the idea that a large group is discussing the person negatively can be damaging to the young tween's psyche.[24] (See lesson 6.11.)

Few people perpetrating the prank want the victim to be really hurt. However, because the idea is formed in the abstract, the victim is not present to show his or her humanity or vulnerability. The potential mob cannot look into the victim's eyes and see a person. It's even more abstract for tweens, who are still developing empathy. The victim remains removed, an abstract notion, and thus, the maliciousness is not checked. The group members, each acting as a singularity in his or her own home, are unaware of the magnitude and impact of the maliciousness. A famous adage is that no single snowflake in an avalanche feels responsible for it. The internet can hide the avalanche of cruelty as the victim is buried under it.

With tweens having limited life experience and less sureness of self to stand up for themselves against mob opinion in their choices, they can be swept up and away by the wave of the online masses urging them to choose to go in a certain direction. Even just in terms of marketing, the internet nudge is bigger and more definitive than the one-on-one suggestion of a friend, and it's far more impersonal, like the force of the moon on tides. How can the internet say something is right for you when they don't know who you are? The tween impulse to follow the crowd can trap them into becoming a lemming running off the cliff. And that's not even considering how many of the likes and recommendations are not real but from *bots*. (See lesson 6.12.)

There is the *too-big sandbox*. As we said at the beginning of the book, there was a time when tweens had their own space, or sandbox, to play in. They were too big for playing with elementary kids yet too immature to hang with teens, let alone adults. Today there is almost no school that even allows tweens and high schoolers to occupy the same recreational space at the same time.

Creating the protected tween space has allowed tweens to gather more age-appropriate information and even practice their own social choice making in the relative safety of a space limited to their peers. It's true that marketers eventually sought out and created many tween-oriented commercial spaces, such as tween-oriented magazines like *J-14* and *Tiger Beat*, but these spaces remained fairly innocuous in discussing subjects like celebrity crushes.[25] Still, most tween interaction, information exchange, and choice making was intratween. A middle-aged guy dressed like a tween and sitting in a tween hangout spot was probably not going to pass.

Now tweens regularly inhabit the online world with anyone and everyone older than they. Social apps declare a minimum age of thirteen to participate, but this is not enforced.[26] Our own surveys, as do most everyone else's, show that tweens are using apps technically designated for older people.[27] Once online, tweens and other minors are in a world where, as they are chatting, gaming, and shopping, many adults with nefarious purposes are specifically seeking out, reaching out, and making contact with them, encouraging tweens to make certain choices.

There are two problems with having one big sandbox. First, tweens are just not ready for that kind of complexity in choosing; there are too many hidden variables in the social calculus. Down in Texas we love football, but no one would think to have middle schoolers, junior varsity, varsity, college, and the pros play on the same field at the same time. Yet online it's one big open field. In consumerism and advertising, seasoned consumers can understand that the "love" of a spokesperson for a product they are recommending has been bought. Many tweens, however, don't yet have the skills to see through the facade to what is actually going on.

The other problem, ironically, has to do with tweens getting bad data as they take in the world. One would think that interacting with more people online in the bigger sandbox would give them a better understanding of socialization dos and don'ts for their own choices, such as what to aspire for. Unfortunately, the samples tweens are getting are skewed. Choices on the internet emphasize more immediate, if ephemeral, rewards, such as celebrity. Yet because the message is pervasive online, it appears complete and definitive.

As we discussed in an earlier chapter, social apps and websites put a premium on *eye candy*, the visually appealing. Most lasting achievement, however, is gained through slow and steady progress, such as the scholar's studious hours, the athlete's hard training, or the artist's determination and perseverance in making a vision real.[28] At most, media depicts effort in a quick montage but with the focus being on the final success. Even the hard work to achieve the glitz, like the hours of prep and touch ups to make someone look "naturally" attractive, is not shown. So tweens see the *pop* of the thousands of likes and conclude that the one final form, usually surface appeal over depth of content, is the best model for success. Choices should be geared to the end result, not the components that lead to the final result. Life is portrayed as a highlight reel of amazing moments and looks. Tweens can find online the amazing two-point slam dunk that everyone oohed over but not the ninety-eight points scored by methodical team play beforehand. In essence, learning about the physical world and what choices one should make by way of the online world can lead to a *sampling error*.[29] (See lesson 6.13.)

NOTES

1. See, Linda Gojak, "Algebra: Not 'If' but 'When'—National Council of Teachers of Mathematics," National Council of Teachers of Mathematics (NCTM), published December 3, 2013, https://www.nctm.org/News-and-Calendar/Messages-from-the-President/Archive/Linda-M_-Gojak/Algebra_-Not-_If_-but-_When_/.

2. He is a character from *Treasure Island*.

3. A man who, by uttering the word "Shazam," became Captain Marvel, a superhero who outsold even Superman comics in the 1940s.

4. She is a character from *A Wrinkle in Time*.

5. He, aka Spider-Man, is the old man of this group at age fifteen in the original comic book.

6. We describe these hormonal and cognitive changes of puberty on tweens more fully in our earlier book *Middle Schoolers, Meet Media Literacy*. We summarize it here because it is so essential to understanding how tweens make choices. Whether IRL twenty years ago or online today, the nature of the tween brain remains the same.

7. There is a third player, the hippocampus, but we are keeping it simple here to minimize what you may have to remember, which actually gives your hippocampus a break.

8. The twenty-five-years threshold has become set in the public mind as a magic fixed number at which adult judgment is acquired and set. Just like height, however, there is no one age at which everyone achieves full maturity. The prefrontal cortex, which does a lot of the heavy lifting in balancing reason and emotion, seems to fully mature *around* twenty-five years of age. Other areas of the brain, such as those that assist in understanding and responding to communication, are also involved.

9. Parents may see this with the sudden mood swings, emotional meltdowns, or even the declarations of "You hate me!" out of nowhere. Kids may experience this in realizing that their parents are now intolerably embarrassing to them in public.

10. Daniel Goleman coined the phrase "amygdala hijack" in his 1995 book, *Emotional Intelligence: Why It Can Matter More than IQ*.

11. See, Rick Ansorge, "Piaget Stages of Development," WebMD, last updated March 12, 2023, https://www.webmd.com/children/piaget-stages-of-development.

12. As budding anthropologists, tweens often give their observed subjects descriptive names like creepy cranky guy or smelly person.

13. This is called FOMO, or fear of missing out.

14. As a general rule of thumb, tween-oriented shows portray adults as clueless or as outwitted by tweens. In contrast, shows geared for teens often have minimal adult characters who are tangentially present or only pop in to give aid or grief to the teens' situation and then fade out.

15. See, David L. Siegel, Timothy J. Coffey, and Gregory Livingston, *The Great Tween Buying Machine: Marketing to Today's Tweens* (Ithaca, NY: Paramount Marketing, 2001).

16. In our own survey of tweens and their internet use, fun was the most cited motivator for being online. When asked what kinds of videos they like to watch, 17 percent of tween respondents specifically used the words "fun" or "funny." Similarly, when asked what was their favorite thing about engaging in social media or watching online videos, 23 percent specifically used the words "fun" or "funny" as part of their favorite thing about any online engagement.

17. Wayback Machine is a popular one.

18. Even worse, tweens have gotten into legal trouble when the emotional comment or photograph that they impulsively post is illegal, such as a threat to someone or a salacious picture of a fellow minor. From a tween's bedroom, they often do not realize that going online is engaging in an interstate mode of communication, and so posting something illegal can be both a state and federal crime.

19. Benedict Carey, "Making Sense of the 'Mob' Mentality," *New York Times*, January 12, 2021, Science, https://www.nytimes.com/2021/01/12/science/crowds-mob-psychology.html.

20. "What Is Swatting? How to Prevent Swatting," Cloudflare, accessed July 15, 2022, https://www.cloudflare.com/learning/security/glossary/what-is-swatting/. One of the most notorious types of malicious pranking is *swatting*, where a gamer and/or a group of gamers who are angry with someone make an anonymous emergency call to police claiming that there is a hostage or another violent tactical situation and gives the target person's address.

21. Who pays for the cost of cleanup or the expenses invoked by the prank?

22. Who wants to be forever marked on the internet as a victim of a prank?

23. "The Truth behind 6 Disturbing Cyberbullying Cases That Turned into Suicide Stories," Washington Township Public Schools, accessed July 15, 2022. https://www.wtps.org /cms/lib8/NJ01912980/Centricity/Domain/745/The%20truth%20 behind%206%20disturbing%20cyberbullying%20cases%20that%20turned%20 into%20suicide.pdf .

24. This has been linked to suicide in youth; for more, see, David D. Luxton, Jennifer D. June, and Jonathan M. Fairall, "Social Media and Suicide: A Public Health Perspective," *American Journal of Public Health* 102, no. S2 (May 2012): S195–200, https://doi.org/10.2105/ajph.2011.300608.

25. Tracie Rozhon, "A Lingerie Maker Returns to Its Racier Past," New York Times, October 25, 2002, https://www.nytimes.com/2002/10/25/business/a-lingerie-maker-returns-to-its-racier-past.html. There were also controversial campaigns that claimed young and underage people were not targeted despite the obvious underage appeal, such as with Victoria's Secrets and their PINK line of garments that launched in 2002.

26. See, Katie Canales, "Silicon Valley Says Kids over the Age of 13 Can Handle the Big, Bad World of Social Media. Experts Say That's the Result of a 'Problematic' 1990s Internet Law," *Business Insider*, January 14, 2022. https://www.businessinsider.com/why-you-must-be-13-facebook-instagram-problematic-law-coppa-2022-1#:~:text=Kids%20will%20be%20exposed %20to%20the%20internet%2C%20regardless%20of%20rules&text=Facebook%20and%20most%20other%20platforms.

27. In our surveys of tweens who regularly go online, social media apps such as Discord, TikTok, and Instagram are popular among tweens who use such apps, despite all three apps having minimum age requirements of thirteen.

28. Thomas Edison, besides getting credit for the lightbulb, should also be acknowledged for persevering through one thousand failed attempts before he got it right.

29. And that's not even addressing more intimate subject matter, such as information about sex on the internet; for more, see, A. M. Hammond, "What Does the Internet Teach Your Teen about Sex?," *Psychology Today*, September 16, 2019, https://www.psychologytoday.com /us/blog/brainstorm/201909/what-does-the-internet-teach-your-teen-about-sex.

Chapter 6 Accompanying Lessons

LESSON 6.1. THE WORLD BETWEEN

Focus of Exploration

Feeling of being a tween.

Intro Questions / Thoughts for Students

Compare how you are now with the version of you three years ago. How has your understanding of the way the world works in terms of good and bad? What would you say to your younger self to give them a truer view of the world? Would you let them keep their view?

Do you feel different about yourself than you did three years ago? Do you feel like you have new powers or abilities of some kind? How so?

Are the stories you read or watch now different from the stories you liked three years ago? How so? Do they deal with more complex issues?

Activity

Think of a story that you know of that involves a kid finding out his life or the greater world is not what he thought it was, with the kid having to confront more complex problems or dangers. For that story write a literary analysis that answers these questions:

- What is the title of the story?
- Describe the main-kid character both in looks and personality.
- What changes happen in his or her world? What new truth does he or she find out?
- What is the new threat or challenge he or she must face?
- Does the kid have any special talents or powers that assist him or her in his or her struggle?
- How does the main character overcome his or her challenges?
- How are adults depicted—good/bad, helpful, or mixed?

After you have done that for the fictional character, think of your own story (or if your life were a story). How would you answer the same questions? Write a literary analysis of your own life (so far!).

Follow-Up Questions/Discussions

Would it surprise you that many kids in middle school feel that their world has changed to reveal a new truth, or that they have some new kind of power? Why do you think few kids talk about it if many feel it?

Many stories are popular because they indirectly are similar to a person's life, at least in terms of feelings. No one is actually teleported to a strange planet, but many kids know what it feels like to move to a strange place they have to adapt to. What are some stories and feelings in those stories that you relate to?

People love the idea of having power, but what are the challenges of having power? If you could have one of the following, which would you choose: super strength, invisibility, the ability to fly, or the power to read people's thoughts? What are the advantages and disadvantages of having each?

Superheroes often have to struggle to hide their superhero powers with another identity. Do you feel like you hide under another identity sometimes? Do you relate to how superheroes struggle to keep up both their hero and other identity at the same time? Can superpowers without the power to turn them off be a curse?

There's a famous old saying that was popularized in *Spider-Man*: "With great power comes great responsibility." What do you think that means? How does that apply to your life?

LESSON 6.2. A SORTED AFFAIR

Focus of exploration

Classification and *seriation*.

Intro Questions / Thoughts for Students

Are you more of a random or an orderly person? A random person is OK with things being out of order and may even like it better. There's a gaming challenge to figuring things out in the moment rather than having them presorted. Orderly people like things neatly arranged and sorted. Even if it takes some effort beforehand, it makes the world more livable and saves time in the long run. In what areas are you each of these? Ask your friends if they agree with you.

When is it OK to rank people from most to least for something about them, like a skill or an attribute? When is it not OK?

Activity

For people you know at school, think about how they are both sorted by circumstances, teachers, or even by themselves into are/aren't types or can/can't abilities. Try to rank the people within those groupings from most to least. For example, you might start with those who like sports and those who do not like sports, and then rank within each how much they seem to like to play.

Now take those groups and think of another attribute and re-sort and re-rank them. For example, change the sorting to be by height—those above and below a certain measure—or those who are good at math, art, or another subject. Don't forget to add yourself into the list!

Follow-Up Questions/Discussions

Sorting (*classification*) and ranking (*seriation*) help us to understand an idea better by seeing the degrees to which it exists, like with an ability. When do you feel like you understand things better if you can arrange them?

The problem with sorting is that we usually are using just one aspect of something to evaluate it, such as height. It can be helpful at times, but why can this also be a trap in one's thinking? Why might that especially be a trap in evaluating people? You may have seen people keep getting regrouped with different people and in a different ranking or order as you re-sorted. What does that tell you about people?

How sure can we be that we know the complete story in evaluating things or people? What hidden abilities or unknown parts of someone's life may not be thought about when people categorize and rank others? We also may not agree on the same definition of a category. For example, a person may not play sports, but they dance for hours and are in great shape. Are they an athlete? Is chess or online gaming a sport? What about being smart?

Are there categories for sorting and ranking at your school or among your friends that you do not like? Why? What can you do, maybe with others, to counter that kind of sorting and ranking?

LESSON 6.3. COLLECT CALL

Focus of Exploration

Messaging about collecting and collections.

Intro Questions / Thoughts for Students

Do you collect anything? What is it? When did you start? What or who first got you into collecting?

Is there anything kids your age collect that you are not into? Why not?

Do you or your friends have any informal collections? You don't usually consider them as a set, but you want a variety of choices. For example, you like having shirts of many colors.

Activity

Look for ads and/or messaging that try to get you to buy a set or collection. It can be a formal set of collectibles or an informal collection, such as offering the product in different types but encouraging you to get them all, like clothes or pens.

Look for how the ads make owning the collection, not just one part, seem great. If you can, analyze the ads with a parent or adult, and ask them if they remember collecting anything.

Follow-Up Questions/Discussions

Which hot collections appeal to you? Which seem boring? People often dismiss collections that don't appeal to them by saying that the collector is paying for stuff to just sit there and be looked at. Is that true, however, for many collections, including perhaps the ones you like?

Why do you think collections are fun? Is it the feeling of accomplishment one gets in having so many? Is it the superiority of having more than others? Is it just the possibility that you could choose from any of them if you wanted? Which part do you like most? Do ads emphasize these positives?

For the ads you saw, did you see any of the following?

- Fast-paced shots (changing a lot) and close-ups of the things to be collected
- Shots of people reacting with amazement and impressed at another's collection
- Several people all playing or interacting together over their shared love of the collectible

What are the messengers trying to say by these shots? Are they true? Make your own ad using these kinds of shots for something totally boring to make it look exciting!

Sometimes ads make it seem like everyone is doing it, so you should too. They try to create a *fad*, or an intense, short-lived excitement for something or some activity. Ask your parents or other adults about fads they remember. Were they glad they did or didn't do it? Why?

Are there nudges or even fads to collect online? How are they similar or different to IRL?

LESSON 6.4. NEWBIE IN TOWN

Focus of Exploration

Being new to something.

Intro Questions / Thoughts for Students

What is a group or activity that you have been doing for a while? Now think back to when you first started, when you were a *newbie*. What do you know now that you didn't know then? What did you think you understood then but now realize you didn't really?

If your present, experienced self could go back and talk to your newbie self from before, what advice would you give? What warnings about traps or choices would you want your newbie self to be aware of? What would you tell your newbie self to do or keep on doing?

Activity

Think of something you are right now a relative newbie at. It can be a group (team) or activity (a play) or situation (school dances). Make lists of three categories: what you know, what you think you know (but maybe want to confirm), and what you don't know but would like to know. Find someone who has experience, and ask them what it was like when they were new. What do they wish they had known? If you feel comfortable, show them all or part of your own list, and ask for their feedback.

Follow-Up Questions/Discussions

Newbies are often afraid to ask because they don't want to look new. They even pretend to know in front of other newbies, when there's a good chance none of the newbies know! Why do people hide their newbie status if everyone is a newbie at some point? Often, experienced people will say their biggest mistake as a newbie was not asking more questions. Is that what you found? If so, why is that a common regret?

In the online gaming world, newbies can sometimes be taken advantage of. Veteran players trick newbies out of gold and gear, even luring their character to a place to rob them within the game. Is this OK if it's just in the game? Do you see this kind of advantage taking in IRL?

Where else do you see how newbies are treated online? Go to a site or chat space where you are a veteran or even an expert. How are newbies treated? If the newbie were a friend of yours, would you like the way they are treated?

Would you do that? If there is something that you don't like about the treatment of newbies, what can you do about it?

Some people who treat newbies badly say it's OK because it's done to everyone or they had to suffer it themselves when they were new. Is that an OK excuse? When does newbie mistreatment become bullying?

LESSON 6.5. PARENTS MUST BE ACCOMPANIED BY A MINOR

Focus of Exploration

Depiction of freedom drivers in media.

Intro Questions / Thoughts for Students

Think back to your favorite shows when you were in second or third grade. How were adults depicted? How were the parents and teachers? Were they present in shows or often absent? Did they know what the kids were up to? How did the adults act, like adults or grown kids?

Activity

Think of shows you like to watch. For a couple of them, watch the show, but imagine you have never seen adults, especially parents, before—like you are a Martian trying to learn about humans by monitoring broadcasts. Based on the examples, what would you conclude about the following?

- How much are adults, especially parents, around or aware of what the kids are up to?
- Are the adults smart? Do they help solve problems, or do the adults need help more from the kids?
- Are the adults good or bad guys? Is this portrayed evenly?
- Do the adults act mature like adults or more like grown kids? How so?

Follow-Up Questions/Discussions

The shows are entertainment geared for kids, but how accurate is the portrayal of adults? Are there adults you can think of that act that way? How do the parents on the show compare to yours or other parents you know IRL?

How does the freedom of kids to do things without adult supervision compare to your own life?

If it doesn't seem realistic, why do shows depict kid life that way? What are the advantages and disadvantages of more freedom at your age?

What is the area or issue in your life when you like adults around to help you the most? What is the area or issue when you want the least help from parents and other adults?

How much do you see adults online? If you limited the word "adult" to people over thirty years old, are there a lot? Is it about the same as IRL? If you were an alien trying to figure out what adult humans were like based just on your online experience, what would you think?

LESSON 6.6. YOU BELONG HERE

Focus of Exploration

Drivers of belonging.

Intro Questions / Thoughts for Students

People like a sense of adventure in exploring something new and different, but they also like feeling comfortable, being in a place they can chill without a lot of effort to recharge. What are examples of places with each of those feelings for you?

Activity

Think of places, activities, or groups of people IRL that you would say you belong to, not in an ownership sense but because you feel "This is me" or "This is my space." What is it about that place, activity, or group that makes you feel that way?

Just as you thought about places, activities, or groups of people IRL that you belong to, think of sites, activities, or groups online that you feel you belong to. What are the online spaces or apps where you relax and feel naturally a part of? Try to express why you feel you belong there in writing or to another person.

Follow-Up Questions/Discussions

Is your feeling of belonging to something online the same as your feeling of belonging to something IRL? How is it the same? How is it different?

Belonging to a group often means excluding some people as not belonging to the group. When can that be a bad thing?

One measure of a group is how they treat others that they don't feel belong to the group. Being in a family doesn't mean it's OK to treat nonfamily members badly. How do the groups you belong to treat nonmembers? What about groups that like something different, such as groups that are big fans of another pop star? If you don't like the way members of your group comment or act toward outsiders, what can you do? Think about what you would want a member of another group to do if someone said bad things about your group or treated you badly.

Is it OK to only want to be in places and with people where you feel you belong? Should you explore places and groups of people where you at first don't think you belong? What can be gained from doing that? What are the risks? Have you ever had to change to a new group, such as changing schools? Overall, was it good or bad to try out new groups and places where at first you did not feel you belonged?

Have you ever seen an advertisement online or IRL that sends the message "You belong here"? How did they send that message? Did they show people who are like you or are doing things you like to do? Did you agree with that message? Why or why not?

LESSON 6.7. IN THE DRIVER'S SEAT

Focus of Exploration

Tween emotional *drivers*.

Intro Questions / Thoughts for Students

As you chose activities in life, what feelings did you want most from your experiences?

Are the positive feelings you get from doing activities IRL the same as for the activities you want or get online? How are they the same, and how are they different?

Activity

Drivers are common positive feelings that kids your age say they like to experience. Kids look for activities or situations that make them feel this way. Four drivers commonly recognized for youth are the feelings of fun, power, freedom, and belonging.

For each of those drivers, think of activities that you do both IRL and online that give you that feeling. If you can't think of one that gives you that feeling in one world, that's OK. Write a short paragraph explaining the activity or situation where you feel that driver and why you feel it there. Also, if there are any other feelings you regularly want to experience, add them to the list. There is one last thing (it may sound strange), but don't overthink the answers. This is an exercise where your gut may be truer and more honest than a long reflection.

Follow-Up Questions/Discussions

We asked you not to think too hard but to go with your gut. That is because, as we discussed in earlier chapters, people have a rational and a nonrational side to making choices. Feelings like having fun are more on the nonrational side. If we think too much, the rational side starts to override or cancel the feelings as we start asking things like "Should we be feeling this?" When, besides in answering surveys, might it also be better to just go with one's gut and block out for the moment the rational side of our brains?

Did you find sources for these feelings in both worlds, IRL and online? Do you find you get some feelings only IRL and some online? Why is that? Do the good feelings you get online more often reinforce good feelings IRL, or do they fill in the gaps by giving you positive experiences and feelings you can't find IRL?

Do the feelings go away as soon as you stop doing the activity, or does it sometimes last a while? Why do you think that is? Do you ever get the positive feeling doing the activity but later have negative feelings like guilt or regret? Why?

Did you add any extra feelings that you seek to have? Do you think those feelings are unique to you or to a few or a lot of kids your age? Our experience is that very few feelings are felt by just one person, and that what one kid does, many do, even if they don't talk about it. Would you be embarrassed if someone knew you liked that feeling or do an activity to feel it?

LESSON 6.8. WHERE OTHERS HAVE GONE BEFORE

Focus of Exploration

Maturation of tastes from tween to teen years.

Intro Questions / Thoughts for Students

Do you like the same things that you liked back in elementary school? For things you don't like as much anymore, which changed more, the thing/activity or you?

What is something you like now that you may not like when you are sixteen? What is something you may like at sixteen that you don't like yet?

Activity

You are going to play the role of a reporter interviewing a retired player about how the game was back when he or she played. The "game," however, is being online, and the veterans are teens.

Find a teenager and ask them to remember what it was like being online when he or she was your age. What did he or she do? What did he or she like and not like about being online "back then"?

As a second part, ask the teen about comparing then and now in two ways:

- How does he think or see the online world has changed for tweens from then to now?
- How has he changed in what he likes doing online then versus now? Did he see that change coming as a tween, or did he just not think about it?

Finally, there are some specific questions you can finish with:

- Can he name something online he thought was funny as a tween? How does that compare to what he finds funny now?
- Does he, looking back, have any regrets about things he did online as a tween? Was there too much of something or not enough of another?
- What advice about being online would he give to his younger tween self—or even to tweens now—if he could?

Be sure to thank the teen for his or her time. If you can, have a discussion with other tweens who did interviews to see if there are common responses by teens.

Follow-Up Questions/Discussions

Did any responses surprise you? Why? Were there any responses that resonated with you? Maybe the teen described doing things as a tween that you do now. Maybe the way he or she said how he or she felt about what was done as a tween made you feel some way.

If the teen does different activities online or doesn't now like what he or she did as a tween, which changed more, the online world or the teen? Could both have changed?

The teen here is acting like an old fashioned scout in the Wild West. He or she is sharing his or her experience so newer people can travel safely. Where else might you benefit from using a "scout" as you start an activity? Where can you be a scout and advise people who are less experienced than you are, such as elementary kids?

Is it OK to like something now even if you know you may not like it when you are older? Is it OK to not like something right now that many older people do like? Should you not worry or be embarrassed and just like what you like? Tweens often want to be like teens, so they imitate them. When is that OK, and when is it better to just enjoy what you like at your age?

LESSON 6.9. FROZEN

Focus of Exploration

Permanency of online postings.

Intro Questions / Thoughts for Students

Think of times you did something potentially embarrassing—we all have them—but where almost no one saw you, or just a friend did, and he or she let it pass. How glad are you that there is no record of it somewhere or that it is only known by a few people?

Is there any past event that occasionally people, often family, bring up that you try to not remember or have discussed? How do you handle that?

Do you have a friend who had a bad day once? Maybe they were mad, or upset, or everything went wrong for them that day. If a third person only knew your friend by that day, would they have a good idea of what your friend was really like?

Activity

We explored before what things you do to get happy, but what do you like to do when you are already happy or in a good mood? What about in a bad mood? Think of activities you do or places you like to go to both IRL and online when you are already in these moods:

- Happy
- Feeling silly
- Sad or depressed
- Angry
- Worried

Follow-Up Questions/Discussions

What if people only knew you by how you've acted in response to negative emotions? What if there was a video of all your actions done IRL when you were sad, angry, and worried? What if the video was available for anyone to see, including a new friend who is first getting to know you or a person who may give you a great job?

If you don't like the idea of a recording of everything you do IRL, what about the things you do online when sad, angry, or worried? Is there anything you have done, such as sending a text, that you are glad only a few people saw? Unfortunately, most every site you go through, including apps, back up their content and activities online. There are programs for seeing how sites looked before. You also might have sent a text, and then, before you could delete it, somebody saw it and even screen captured it.

Ask older people who text which they regret more when looking back, things they posted or things they didn't post? When they regret having posted something, what was their mood when they posted? It doesn't even have to be a negative feeling. Sometimes people post what they think is funny at the moment but later regret it. Ask about that.

Given the risk of freezing your reputation by a single bad or thoughtless post or online activity, what can you do? IRL, some people advise to take a beat, count to ten, or sleep on it before reacting. Pause, think, and let the negative feelings cool down first. Can you do this online? Can you put a warning or reminder to yourself on your computer or phone to tell you to pause (like a cat's *paws*)?

We should end this negative-feeling discussion by going back to your positive emotions. After you have done something that creates or continues positive emotions, the feeling may be gone, but the memory of the positive feeling remains. What can you do to keep that positive feeling or memory of it with you? Ask people what they carry to remind them of good times and feelings. Maybe make a survey of what people carry with them. What do you carry with you to remind you to carry positive feelings or the memory of them? If you carry positive emotions, they can return the favor and carry you at times!

LESSON 6.10. AG-GREGATE

Focus of Exploration

Echo chambers and identities.

Intro Questions / Thoughts for Students

What is something you loved four or five years ago? It can be a lunch you ate every day or a band or a game. Try to think of something that they used to say: "I am team _____!"

What is something your parents or other adults remember you were a very devoted fan of? Again, it could be food, an activity, or anything.

For the thing you were so attached to or were devoted to, how did you feel about people who liked something different? Did you ever dislike them for liking something different?

Activity

Think of something you really like now. It can be IRL, online, or both. For that thing, you are going to be an anthropologist who studies the "AG" (affinity group) of those who also like it. Try to just observe and make observations about it:

- How does the AG identify each other? Do they have certain clothing or slang words they use to identify that they are members?
- Does the AG ask for anything to be given up or given to the group to be a member?
- How open is the AG to new members? Is there an initiation?
- How flexible is the AG? Are there different degrees of liking? Is it okay to be in the AG on a casual basis? Can a person drop out for a bit and then rejoin without a problem?
- How does the group treat members of AGs that like something else or who don't like what the group likes? Is the AG friendly or hostile to other groups?

Follow-Up Questions/Discussions

What are your reasons for liking the AG and being a member? Are there reasons beyond everyone liking the same thing? Do your connections with group members go beyond that?

You like the thing or activity your AG is organized around, but how much do you generally like the way the AG acts about it? Is there anything the AG says or does that you do not like? As a group member, how can you change that? Are there others who feel the same way?

Are there members of the group who have other interests or like other things maybe even more? Are there members that this is the only thing they care about? How do they feel about people who are just casually involved or who belong to other AGs too?

Are you friends with nonmembers of the AG? When does your AG membership not matter? Are there any times when others say it does matter, but you think it should not?

Are there conflicts between your AG and other AGs? Do you feel more tied to the group when they have a conflict with outsiders? Does anything positive come from the conflict?

Is there a difference between AGs you belong to IRL and online? Are your online AGs an extension of groups IRL or different? How so? Do online AGs act differently than ones IRL?

Are you now friends with anyone who was in a different AG a couple of years ago? What does that tell you about AGs?

LESSON 6.11. MOBBING RULE

Focus of Exploration

Mobbing.

Intro Questions / Thoughts for Students

Have you ever felt pressured to do something or make a choice because a group of people, such as your friends, all seemed to be nudging you to go one way?

Have you ever told a friend or another person that they were pressuring you too much? How do you tell them to stop nudging or pressuring you? Did it work? If it didn't, what did you do? Did you just walk away? Did you get support for resisting?

Activity

For emergency situations, we often make a plan beforehand. It saves time and helps us to act when our emotions might cloud our thinking. We put a priority on getting out to a safe place.

Almost everyone can recall being pressured by an individual or a large group of people to make a choice. It can be intense and overwhelming. So why don't we have a plan ahead of time?

With some friends, come up with a pressure drill to use when faced with a large nudge to make a choice you might be hesitant to make. Your plan should include the following:

- What are the recognizable signs that a bad situation is coming or happening?
- What can you do to try to stop the situation from getting out of control? What can you say or do to turn the situation around, like "I need time to think"?
- If the situation gets out of control, or even before that, what is an exit strategy to get to safety? How can you get out?
- What can others who see the situation do to help stop the situation or get people out?
- Whom should you notify of the problem?

Follow-Up Questions/Discussions

This exercise may sound silly, but the fact is that you will probably encounter pressure or negative situations from teasing to bullying to *mobbing*. It's best to prepare.

Unlike a fire drill, where the person is reacting as a victim, you should also discuss what to do if you are in the group that is pressuring. Just as a fire gets out of control, an incident of teasing or bullying can get bigger and beyond the intent of the individuals who started it. How can you look out for a situation blowing up? How can you get others to be aware?

With a fire the warning is a bell or even the word "Fire!" For feeling pressured, perhaps you can come up with a word or signal to your friends that says you need help in a situation.

Online there may be distance between you and the mob, as they are not in your face. On the other hand, there can be so many more people, and it's all public. You can even feel pressure at home, alone. How can you plan to resist when the mob or other pressure is online?

LESSON 6.12. RECOMMENDED JUST FOR YOU

Focus of Exploration

Online recommendations, trustworthiness of internet group opinion.

Intro Questions / Thoughts for Students

When you consider choosing something, how much do you look at or listen to recommendations as to what to choose? For what kinds of things do you check out what other people think? What about reviews by others—when do you trust more reviews by friends and when by the experts?

Do you ever look at online reviews, and if so, for what kinds of things? How are they better than and not as good as getting recommendations IRL?

Activity

Pick a product, activity, or place you are interested in checking out. Look at the recommendations and reviews online. Most product sites have reviews. Google has reviews of places too.

- Do you see any patterns in the reviews, such as a particular part of the product or service is praised or criticized? Is there any similar language?
- What can you tell by looking at the date of the reviews? Why might the date be important?
- What can you tell about the balance of good and bad reviews? What can you conclude overall?

You might want to do some research about fake reviews on sites, and then see if you can spot any potential ones.

Follow-Up Questions/Discussions

How specific were the reviews? Did they say "great" or "terrible," or did they give specific examples of what was great and terrible? Does that make a difference in influencing you? Was there a difference in specificity between positive and negative reviews?

Which do you trust more, the opinion of a close friend who knows you or the collective opinion of a lot of people who may not know you? Why?

If we know that many reviews and ratings are faked or, in other ways, are not real, can they still be helpful in our choosing? How? How can you spot fake reviews, either from their paying people to post positive reviews or using bots? If a site or person uses fake reviews to seem more liked, is that lying?

Some people leave malicious reviews. They are mad, often for another reason entirely, but they channel their anger by leaving a public bad review so as to hurt. Is that OK? If a friend said they were going to do that, what might you say to them?

Do you think people take the time to leave a review more when they are happy or unhappy with it? Do you voice your opinion more about things when you are happy or unhappy about it? Does that match the balance of good and bad reviews you find online?

Have you ever left a review? This would be a good time to do so. Be thoughtful and fair.

LESSON 6.13. SAMPLING ERROR?

Focus of Exploration

Sampling error. Representation of life on internet, depiction of gender online.

Intro Questions / Thoughts for Students

How accurate do you think the online world is at portraying the world IRL? People often watch TV shows and say, "That's not real life!" What do you think about how the real world is shown online?

Think of 9:30 a.m. this morning. What were you doing? If someone saw that one minute, could they accurately know or guess what the rest of your day would be like? Why or why not?

Activity

Watch videos, play games, chat, or do your usual activities online. However, pretend you know nothing of the world IRL, that you are an alien trying to get an idea of human society by monitoring the online world (which can be picked up in space). For each category, write a general assessment of what you learned about human men and women. If you want to get more detailed, you can subdivide categories, such as making lists of the jobs you see men and women doing. Use table 6.1.

Table 6.1. Human Observation Notes

	Men	Women	Other or Not Sure
Looks			
Clothing			
Jobs and role in society			
Personalities			
Skills			
Athletics			
Hobbies and interests			
Other			

Looks—Do you see a wide variety of different looks, including body shapes and faces?

Clothing—What do humans wear? How much do different people cover up or expose, and what seems to be the message of the clothing?

Jobs and role in society—If a person has a job, what kind is it? Is it one of the mind, working with hands, or taking care of others?

Personalities—Are they fun and joking or serious? Do they interact with others, or are they more on their own?

Skills—What skills do they possess? Do men/women/others have about equal skills? Does one seem to have more of a particular kind of skill?

Athletics—Who are the athletes, and what are men's and women's sports? Are they equal?

Hobbies and interests—When they are chilling, what are they doing?

Other—Is there anything else that jumps out at you?

Follow-Up Questions/Discussions

Did you find the online representation overall to be accurate? What about as regarding men, women, and others? Were the things shown how you understand the real world to be? If not, why does the online world depict it that way?

Did you think about cultures outside of your own? Did you find more representations of a culture from one country or part of the world? Did you see a wide variety of all the world cultures? Why do you think that is?

You also have to check yourself. Could it be that there are more and different depictions, but your choice of places to visit are not representative? This is not a criticism of you, but every investigator (including us!) needs to be aware of his or her own sampling bias. It could be *both* the online world and where you chose to go had *sampling errors*. What can you do to test your observations and results? In the science world, people ask others to repeat their investigations to compare results. Can you do that here?

No doubt there are many kinds of different people, but they are not all depicted equally. Just like IRL, a scientist who is busy in the lab may not get his or her picture published as much as an actor or celebrity. Why is that? Is it the same online? How can you find the same kind of unrepresented people online?

If you decided that the online world does not represent IRL, does it make you wonder if, even though you know a lot, there is still more information, more variety of choices, that you do not know about? How can you find out?

Chapter Seven

Millennial, Gen Z, and Gen A Life

What's the biggest misconception by the older generation about the younger generation? It's thinking the younger generation is so radically different from them. And what's the biggest misconception that the younger generation has about the older generation? It's thinking that the older generation is so radically different from them.

American pop sociology likes to divide ages into generations by birth year in groups of about fifteen to twenty years (see lesson 7.1):

- Boomers—born from 1945 to 1964
- Gen X—born from 1965 to 1979
- Gen Y (millennials)—born from 1980 to 1995
- Gen Z—born from 1996 to 2009
- Gen A—born from 2010 to 2024 or so

In some ways it is easier to understand an individual's perspective by knowing when he was born or the circumstances under which she matured, such as his or her birth order.[1] Like any *heuristic*, however, we need to be aware of the limits and exceptions to categorical lumping. One of the authors here was born as a very late boomer,[2] but as the fourth and youngest child, he grew up in the boomer culture of his siblings. He has friends the same age, however, who grew up as the oldest child and feel themselves more tied with Gen X. The other author, four years younger, would be considered a Gen Xer along with her three younger siblings. Still, any categorization based on American generations is thrown off, as she was born and raised in another country—Thailand—with entirely different experiences growing up.[3]

Some older people today often assume that all Gen Z folks are digital "natives" and take being online for granted. Meanwhile, we need to remember that 25 percent of households in the United States do not have internet access.[4]

That doesn't mean we shouldn't look at and consider the different circumstances each generation faces from a general point of view. It's like studying the general water quality while still recognizing that there are different kinds of fish in different kinds of water.

In comparing Gen Y—millennials—and Gen Z, it's often hard for older folks to tell them apart.[5] Comparing millennials and Gen Z in any given year is problematic because they are in different stages in life. During the great recession of 2007–2009, older millennials were job seeking, while a good portion of Gen Z was still in school. A 2019 Canadian study found that a top motivation for consuming cultural content online for millennials was to find out places for food and drinks, while for Gen Z, it was gaming.[6] Is this because the two generations have different values or because they are at different stages in life? For both millennials and Gen Z, as well as the new kids of Gen Alpha, the pandemic and the impact of the resulting lockdown at their stage of life will no doubt define a generational memory. (See lessons 7.2 and 7.3.)

Much of the millennial/Gen Z demarcation (or with any other demographic) is done by groups who have a specific interest or purpose. Academics divide by age-groups to study more precise impacts. Marketers like to separate generations to target their interests or to puff up new consumers with messages that effectively say, "Don't listen to the old folks telling you it's a bad deal. It's a new era, so be independent, and buy it for yourself!"[7]

We demarcate millennials and Gen Z by media exposure and consumption. Millennials will remember youth-oriented media as kids' cable TV channels at the turn of the millennium. The 1990s were a watershed decade, as it was the unleashing of massive advertising directly to kids. Nickelodeon, Disney, and Cartoon Network commanded attention as both the principal entertainers and the messengers to youth. The world of choice had opened up for kids because, instead of a few networks setting aside a small portion of airtime for children's programming, now there was a wide range of offerings for kids to choose from twenty-four hours a day. Apart from TV, millennials may also remember archaic outings to a Blockbuster video store or excitedly getting a DVD from the new company Netflix *in the mail*.

Gen Zers were still young when cable TV hit a high point in the early 2000s. They were just behind the tween media peak that witnessed *High School Musical*, *iCarly*, *Hannah Montana*, and other tween-oriented shows. Older Gen Zers came into tween years as cable's popularity was beginning to wane. More appealing to the Gen Z was streaming online, with Netflix becoming the giant of the new medium. Streaming offered more choice—which is what this book is all about—as one could pick a particular program to watch at any given time. In 2006, laptops, offering more personal and moveable viewing, began to consistently outsell desktop computers.[8]

The biggest generational media change, as one would expect, has been the internet. So much could be written, so let's boil it down to some key points. Whereas the internet was initially a novelty for early millennials and then slowly became integrated more and more into their lives, for Gen Z, it was a predominant force for as long as they can remember.[9] By 2002 over 50 percent of the population claimed to use the internet.[10] The other tectonic shift occurred on January 9, 2007. There had been "smartphones" that had allowed connection with the internet going back to ten years before, as well as Blackberries and PalmPilots, but Apple's introduction of the iPhone brought the internet into the palms of the masses' hands. For those who could afford it, it made for a connection that was always on, always accessible, and always creating a messaging system both outward and inward. Some people have been connected, never alone with their own thoughts, ever since.[11]

It is this approximate decade, from 2002 to 2013, in which Gen Z and many millennials distinguish between what is called *old media* and *new media*. Old media is generally broadcast and is inherently for mass consumption. Whether it is movies or TV, programmers either try to figure out what appeals to the greatest number of viewers or target a specific but large demographic, and they then provide content that consumers choose to take or leave. New media, on the other hand, is considered more personalized and interactive. It is more niche tailored, more diverse, and is often driven more by consumer personal choice and demand as to content. If consumers can switch between a multitude of other choices on the web or streaming with a simple click, then content providers have pressure to give consumers what they want and be more intimate and personal. The introduction of apps also allowed new media to be more two-way, with consumers able to voice their choice and even bend content to their collective will. It's a new take on the old economic concept of consumer sovereignty.[12]

Unfortunately, the media may be new and even more truly responsive and personal to consumers, but that doesn't mean the power has been shifted to be with a consumer's choice. Consumers, even in the new media, are swayed and nudged to make choices that they have been told is what they "want" by earlier media, such as having to get the hot brand or watching the popular influencer,[13] lest they suffer FOMO.

Marketers also can be deceitful even in the just-for-you, personal-choice genre of the internet. Content providers will make videos that seem intimate for their followers, with the influencer in bed, stage whispering a secret they want only their fans to know. It feels personal, especially when watching content on a laptop or phone in one's room rather than in a family room with others. One should realize, however, that the influencer in bed sharing a spontaneous moment "just woke up" with perfect makeup and hair or that there are forced mentions or placement of a brand name in the clip. The whisperer may not even be alone in the room, as there may be someone to record, another for sound, and another to hold up the cue cards for the influencer to read the from-the-heart message. And all of it is going out, personally, to the one hundred thousand fans, "just for them." (See lesson 7.4.)

The internet is no worse than old media in depicting fake intimacy, except that the consumers, alone in their rooms, may feel like it is more personal because they see the video when and where they wish and on their terms.

One misunderstanding, if not deception, that is different between old and new media is about who the consumers actually are. Viewers of new media may believe they are the ultimate end user, the buyers, even if they don't pay anything. What they may not realize is that the actual paying audiences are the companies that pay for the data extracted by the app or website from its viewers. It's like the mice thinking the lab is all set up for them because they get a nice bit of cheese at the end of the maze. They don't realize that the cameras, the constant observations, and measurements of them are not for their benefit but for the observers. And what is there to do if the mice won't cooperate? Well, there's always other mice.[14]

Gen Z and Gen A have shown a clear preference for videos.[15] Netflix, with its large but still limited variety of movies (chosen or retired by Netflix) as well as with its fees for streaming, is struggling as of this writing. What has emerged as the new media forces are TikTok, YouTube, and other platforms for short videos made by professionals, amateurs, and professionals trying to look like amateurs. It is definitely more democratized and diverse, as anyone can upload content. Videos can be instantly shared, liked, or commented upon. Viewers can even reach out to the *content creator* by way of a comment, posted email address, or other link.[16] It is a two-way communication in which viewers can actively engage with the content creator, unlike with Netflix.

Both our own survey of tweens and those of others have identified humor as a top draw for video viewing.[17] Researcher Patricia West found that people of all ages and circumstances have trouble elucidating their preferences or reasons for their choices.[18] It's an intuitive preference that often defies description. West found, however, that isolating features can make such preferences more definite and subject to analysis and, ultimately, be a reflection by the people making the choices. (See lessons 7.5 and 7.6.)

GEN A

The newest identifiable age-group, Gen A, are now the heart of tweendom. Millennials, now looking to move up company ladders and plan family vacations for their kids, are nearing irrelevancy to youth marketing, except as parents.

How is life and choice making different for Gen A, especially online? Data is a bit sparse because, technically, they are supposedly too young to be on most apps due to the thirteen-year age minimum. There are also laws, like COPPA,[19] that ban sites like YouTube from collecting data on users under thirteen.

What we can know is that millennials dabbled with the internet and made room in their otherwise physical world for it, and Gen Z was more comfortable with being online nearly from the beginning. Gen A, so far, is one that lives in the dual worlds of physical and online experience, making choices in both realms simultaneously.[20]

Every generation, as we said before, has defining or lifestyle-altering events. Many millennials will compare life before and after 9/11. The first Gen Zers came into tweendom as the great recession of 2007 hit and were seeing the upheaval, economic downturn, and bitter political polarization afterward.

To date, the defining event for Gen A has been the COVID-19 pandemic and lockdown. It will take years to get the full picture, but we know how important being online immediately became for them. For Gen Z being online was an extra part of education and life. For many in Gen A, being online was their lifeline to school; to friends; and to being, in most ways, still a part of society. The balance of the two worlds and the consequences of choosing tilted toward the online one.

The technology and lockdown circumstances have imbued Gen A with a familiarity with and passion for the virtual never before seen. That makes them more comfortable in making choices about what they consume or do online. They are able to maximize the online world for the best it has to offer. Unfortunately, because they are so familiar with the online world, they also drop their caution and may be prone to easy misinformation and misadventure in making choices, especially given that they still operate cognitively in a concrete, one might say naive, manner. (See lessons 7.7 and 7.8.)

Given Gen A's skew to living online, we think it appropriate to end a book on youth choices by summarizing the nature of choice making online for them.[21] In many ways, the same techniques of cost-benefit analysis previously examined apply equally online and IRL. Still, there are some extra considerations for choice making for youth that teachers, parents, and other people guiding them in making smart choices need to be aware of.

THE ONLINE WORLD *IS* A REAL WORLD FOR YOUTH

Oldsters have a verbal habit of referring to things that happen outside of the internet as the "real world" in a way that implies what happens online should be discounted or is of less substance or impact. It implies to youth that they should not let what they experience online affect them as much. Their choices have ephemeral consequences.

For today's youth, however, the online world is at least as real and impactful as the physical world. Tweens can have many online social relationships and sometimes even more than they have in the physical world. They may feel more affinity with people they know online and get the bulk of their entertainment and information from the online world, especially those socially marginalized IRL. Certainly, tweens see how much adults themselves integrate the online world, such as making purchases, getting news, keeping in touch with friends, and even finding life partners. They also experience teachers using and directing students toward the internet as an essential part of their education.

Tweens are actually more aware of what's going on in the real world than previous generations in large part from being online. They will step into adulthood with more choices already laid out, if not predetermined, from online acculturation. Many are also more directly engaged even as youth. Adult critics call it *slacktivism*, the idea of supporting movements and causes online, because, to such critics, it seems like nothing is actually done except voicing digital support. However, studies show youth awareness of issues leads to greater choices by them to take action, whether directly in the real world or through the internet, which then leads to tangible results.[22]

TWEENS ARE MORE AWARE OF THE CHOICES AND ACTIONS ADULTS MAKE THAN IN YEARS BEFORE

When the internet was first popularized in the 1990s, visionaries excitedly anticipated a general improvement for society in terms of information access. Certainly, this has been realized by those who can investigate the world or answer a question with a simple query. What was overly optimistic, however, was the anticipation that people with particular or already-decided views would choose to listen to each other, including to those with opposing views, and then evolve their thinking in a peaceful and collaborative manner.

Tweens today have grown up in a society where people are more politically polarized than before.[23] Adult exhortation that public discourse wasn't always this divisive, whether that's true or not, is irrelevant to youth today. They see the choices adults make and believe that is the way of things. Adults contest issues in the public forum of the internet, where people are not afraid to share more vitriol. What is often modeled for youth is not a good-faith exchanging of views but the use of *fallacies* and personal attacks rather than reason and facts in promoting their side. Perhaps worse, many actively and intentionally seek to not solve but merely disrupt. We tell kids to work out differences and not get personal, but then kids see *discussion threads* overtaken by *trolling*.[24] Given youth's aspirational motivation, it becomes the model for their choices. (See lessons 7.9 and 7.10.)

YOUTH ARE OVERWHELMED BY THE INFORMATION THEY ARE SUPPOSED TO CONSIDER IN MAKING CHOICES

The greatness with webs is that everything is connected. It can also be a problem. The online world with all its interconnected information can be a massive data dump on youth, who are just emerging from linear investigations of life. The information overload is too much even for tweens in the *concrete operational stage*, trying to seriate and classify all aspects of life. How can one calculate a good resulting product when all the factors to be multiplied are too great to keep in mind?

A good example is the issue of internet privacy. Tweens are leaving the kiddie pool of elementary years to start wading into the great ocean of worldwide connection. They have eager and innocent excitement, even while adults around them scream about sharks looking to harvest data from them and otherwise do unseen harm. The tween, who probably isn't even fully understanding of the abstract concept of personal data, can be overwhelmed by tales of how data extraction could somehow hurt them in some indirect or future way, when all they want to do is play a game on Roblox or watch a two-minute TikTok video. They also see friends, family, and others moving about freely and not seeming to worry much about data thieves. For tweens already looking to push away from parents, all the warnings and admonitions become discountable background noise to their choices.

THE HALLMARK OF INTERNET CHOICE MAKING FOR YOUTH IS "AUTHENTICITY"

When youth try to identify why they choose to watch an influencer or video clip, aside from humor, one word often recurs: *authenticity*.[25] There's no doubt it is an offshoot of the nihilism young people feel from seeing the disingenuous messaging of adults online. They have been thrown into a sandbox online with people of all ages, who act with a wide variety of honesty and good intent. Perhaps they miss the simpler, smaller sandbox of childhood, where one doesn't have to spend energy worrying if the promises and guarantees were actually meant. The desire for authenticity is so persuasive, business magazines like *Forbes* oxymoronically exhort salespeople to appear so and give tips to would-be influencers on how to "keep it real" by making one's online presence more authentic.[26]

What is being authentic online? It's giving—or at least appearing to be giving—your honest opinion rather than one you think is popular or serves you best. It's also not *posing*, or pretending to be something you are not to fool others. Tweens of parents who try to use kid slang will tell you it's painful.[27] Of course, what naive youth may not realize is the preparation that goes into spontaneous authenticity. For marketers and influencers, their analytics tell them that honest opinion is already a popular one that will be well received. It's dressing how you want to dress, though it just happens that how you want to dress is the latest killer look. It's an influencer not saying something just to sell, though their opinion can be expressed while holding a drink, making sure the label is out as the drink makers requested he do.[28] To be fair, many adults as well can't tell what true authenticity is. That's why such marketing works on all ages!

One consequence of the search for authenticity is how it impacts tween desire for classification in choice making. Tweens will stick with an influencer because the influencer has been classified as authentic. Once an influencer is designated as authentic or of good character, tween opinion of the online personality is *anchored*. They will overlook any indication otherwise. Tweens will forgive even serious transgressions committed by the influencer as long as the influencer appears to sincerely apologize and remain authentic.[29] If the influencer is determined to be inauthentic, however, then young kids are quick to turn away.[30] (See lesson 7.11.)

NOTES

1. One study, for example, shows that eldest children responded more to marketing appeals invoking social-conscious responsibility than younger siblings. See, Tobias Otterbring and Michał Folwarczny, "Firstborns Buy Better for the Greater Good: Birth Order Differences in Green Consumption Values," *Personality and Individual Differences* 186 (February 2022): 111353, https://doi.org/10.1016/j.paid.2021.111353.

2. They are sometimes called generation Jones.

3. We, the authors, have two children, a son born in 1995 and another son born in 1996, but it would be inaccurate to say they are two different generations by just going strictly by the year designations indicated above.

4. Catherine McNally, "Nearly 1 in 4 Households Don't Have Internet—and a Quarter Million Still Use Dial-Up," Reviews.org, published August 17, 2021, https://www.reviews.org /internet-service/how-many-us-households-are-without-internet-connection/.

5. Personal remembrance of the September 11, 2001, attacks are often used as a delineation point.

6. Vice Media, "The Culture of Content Consumption," published August 2019, https://ontariocreates.ca/uploads/Business_Intelligence/en/GENZ_The_Culture_of_Content_Consumption.pdf.

7. Then again, it's every generation's right, if not duty, to be silly and frivolous in its own way. Ask an oldster about the pet rocks of the 1970s.

8. Charles Arthur, "How Laptops Took over the World," *The Guardian*, October 28, 2009, https://www.theguardian.com/technology/2009/oct/28/laptops-sales-desktop-computers#:~:text=In%20the%20US%2C%20laptops%20first.

9. Again, this is bearing in mind that not everyone has the luxury or privilege of internet access.

10. "Internet Penetration United States 2017," Statista, published 2017, https://www.statista.com/statistics/209117/us-internet-penetration/.

11. "Mobile Fact Sheet," Pew Research Center, published April 7, 2021, https://www.pewresearch.org/internet/fact-sheet/mobile/. The year 2013 was the watershed year when over 50 percent of Americans said they owned a smartphone.

12. Consumer sovereignty is a general idea that as between sellers and buyers (consumers), buyers have more of an ability to walk out of a store and go somewhere else. That gives them more independence and power in negotiating a price. Of course, many factors, such as alternate availability, brand loyalty, and media nudging, also affect how much sovereignty consumers actually have.

13. *Influencers* are people with large cultural nudging power. They are often today found online and are addressed in detail in our companion book to this, *The Social Media Diet*.

14. The issues of privacy, data extraction, and explaining it to youth is touched upon in our companion book, *The Social Media Diet*, but that's our little secret with you.

15. As of this book, the demand and trend are so clear that once picture-based apps like Instagram are moving to incorporate more videos (*reels*) in response to generational preferences.

16. Whether the content provider actually reads it is not really the point. The link to communicate empowers the viewers and gives them the feeling of input and connection.

17. Vice Media, "The Culture of Content Consumption," published August 2019, https://ontariocreates.ca/uploads/Business_Intelligence/en/GENZ_The_Culture_of_Content_Consumption.pdf.

18. Patricia M. West, Christina L. Brown, and Stephen J. Hoch, "Consumption Vocabulary and Preference Formation," *Journal of Consumer Research* 23, no. 2 (September 1996): 120, https://doi.org/10.1086/209471.

19. Federal Trade Commission, "Children's Online Privacy Protection Rule ('COPPA')," published July 25, 2013, https://www.ftc.gov/legal-library/browse/rules/childrens-online-privacy-protection-rule-coppa.

20. Studies in the last couple of years are showing that the brain operates in a more multitasking state while we are online. Repeatedly operating in that mode can have an impact on how our brains then operate even when we are not online, adversely affecting attention and short-term memory. See, Rawan Tarawneh, "How Does the Internet Affect Brain Function?," The Ohio State University Wexner Medical Center, published February 26, 2020, https://wexnermedical.osu.edu/blog/how-internet-affects-your-brain#:~:text=Recent%20research%20suggests%20that%20excess.

21. And did we mention there is a companion book to this one that focuses just on online choice making—*The Social Media Diet*?

22. Sonya Friel, "Modern-Day Youth Activism: Youth Engagement in the Digital Age," *Global Fund for Children*, September 9, 2021, https://globalfundforchildren.org/story/modern-day-youth-activism-youth-engagement-in-the-digital-age/. Part of the difficulty in measuring the translation of digital activism into physical activism was the interruption of physical engagement due to COVID-19 and the responding lockdowns. More time and data will be needed to have a better understanding of the relationship between digital and physical volunteerism.

23. "Political Polarization in the American Public," Pew Research Center, published June 12, 2014, https://www.pewresearch.org/politics/2014/06/12/political-polarization-in-the-american-public/.

24. In a series of interviews with millennials and Gen Zers, there was a repeated distaste expressed for discussion threads that were hijacked by trolls, who then reduced the thread to gratuitous attacks. Many cited this as their reason for preferring limited chat groups over general-discussion apps like Facebook.

25. Nichole Howson, "Why Being Authentic on Social Media Is Important," AIM Social, published October 27, 2018, https://aimsmmarketing.com/why-being-authentic-on-social-media-is-important/#:~:text=Being%20Authentic%20helps%20create%20a.

26. Leslie Licano, "Council Post: Keeping It Real: The Importance of Having an Authentic Social Media Presence," *Forbes*, September 13, 2019, https://www.forbes.com/sites/forbesagencycouncil/2019/09/13/keeping-it-real-the-importance-of-having-an-authentic-social-media-presence/?sh=44353f37110f.

27. An interesting case of posing is how old media is trying to pose as new media. Old media will try to make memes popular with youth or start online chats about their content, such as a movie. If the youth catch on to the promo, usually done when seeing how forced and inauthentic the push is, the campaign will backfire. See, Emma Wallenbrock, "Hordes of Teens in Suits Are Showing Up to the Minions Movie. The Studio, for Once, Did the Right Thing," *Slate*, July 7, 2022, https://slate.com/culture/2022/07/minion-rise-of-gru-box-office-gentleminions-meme.html.

28. In one video an influencer sent a personal message to her followers that she is being compelled to do a jingle that will come out later for a company. She wanted her fans to know that she hates making jingles and that when the jingle for the company does come out, know that she didn't want to do it. It's a great stealth promo because it builds anticipation for the "real ad" to come for the company that is repeatedly named (and thus promoted) in the pre-ad disclaimer video. The influencer gets to keep her appearance of authenticity by denouncing it; the company gets both a pre-ad and an ad. The jingle will also now be focused on and inculcated.

29. Claire Rutter, "PewDiePie Begs for Forgiveness for Victims of Offensive Prank," *Mirror*, January 17, 2017, https://www.mirror.co.uk/3am/celebrity-news/pewdiepie-begs-forgiveness-victims-offensive-9635474. Pewdiepie is a world-famous influencer who has, at times, gone too far even by his own admission, especially after there has been backlash and fallout. His fans remain loyal, however, and one can see explanations of fan forgiveness in chat forums. See, DeadricBaguette, "Why was Pewdiepie so easily forgiven for saying the n word?," Reddit, February 5, 2022, https://www.reddit.com/r/ask/comments/slb4lw/why_was_pewdiepie_so_easily_forgiven_for_saying/?sort=new.

30. Elaine Wallace et al., "Do Brand Relationships on Social Media Motivate Young Consumers' Value Co-Creation and Willingness to Pay? The Role of Brand Love," *Journal of Product & Brand Management* 31, no. 2 (June 15, 2021): 189–205, https://doi.org/10.1108/jpbm-06-2020-2937. See also, Maren Becker, Nico Wiegand, and Werner J. Reinartz, "Does It Pay to Be Real? Understanding Authenticity in TV Advertising," *Journal of Marketing* 83, no. 1 (December 4, 2018): 24–50, https://doi.org/10.1177/0022242918815880.

Chapter 7 Accompanying Lessons

LESSON 7.1. TALKIN' 'BOUT THEIR GENERATION

Focus of Exploration

Generational similarities and differences.

Intro Questions / Thoughts for Students

Think of the adults in your life. Try to picture them when they were your age. Do you see them as just a younger version of themselves now? Can you imagine them as different, a typical kid?

Are there any feelings, thoughts, or concerns you think that kids your age have that previous generations of kids didn't experience?

Activity

Interview several adults, hopefully of various ages, about life when they were your age. You can use the questions below or come up with your own:

- What year were you the questioner's age?
- What was the feel of that time? What was life like for you?
- What was the big issue or news of the day generally?
- What was society like for people of your gender? Was there a distinction between people of different genders?
- What were the biggest issues that concerned you in your life?
- What did you and your friends like to do for fun? What games or activities did you like? Why did you like doing it?
- When were you happiest?
- How did you feel about adults back then?
- What did adults say about your generation back then?

Follow-Up Questions/Discussions

In comparing generations, we often look at things like technology that kids have used, such as television versus the internet. However, are kids of different times still basically the same? Why or why not? Can the different technologies be seen as doing the same thing, like connecting kids with the world? Why or why not? When is the difference so great that they cannot be compared?

Can different news stories at different times still affect kids in similar ways? For example, kids long ago may have been very concerned about nuclear war; today they are concerned about climate change. Can the two be seen as similar in worrying kids about world calamity?

Are there any issues of the past that are still around for kids today, such as discrimination? If so, how has it changed? Do kids think about the issue the same way? Why or why not?

If something is discussed or done more today than in past times, does that mean it was not an issue or on people's minds before? Which ideas or activities are new? Which do you think may have been around but weren't discussed as much?

LESSON 7.2. ONCE IN A GENERATION

Focus of Exploration

Events that shape or define a generation.

Intro Questions / Thoughts for Students

Think of big historical events that happened in the last one hundred years, such as the Great Depression, World War II, or the moon landing. It could also be a long-standing issue, like the Cold War. How do you think that event affected kids growing up during it? Did it directly affect them, such as having shortages of things? How did it affect them emotionally? Did it make them worried or hopeful? Try to imagine yourself during that time.

Can big world news affect how kids see life? Can it make them overall a positive or worried generation? Can it change what they value? Can you think of an example?

Activity

List out some big news events or issues in your life. For those events, write out how they directly changed your life and the lives of people your age. What increased and what decreased because of it?

Try to then determine how those events changed the attitude or outlook of kids your age. Did it make your generation happy and positive or sad and worried? Why?

Follow-Up Questions/Discussions

Do the events affect all kids your age equally, or do they affect certain groups of people more than others? Why?

Often, the impact on lives is not the event but the response to the event afterward. Have the responses to your events affected you or people you know? How?

How many of the things you listed were good events, and how many were bad? Does that tell you whether we remember good or bad more?

Were the things you named the introduction of new technology? We sometimes don't see the impact of technology until later, such as how the introduction of the smartphone changed life. Is there any small, new technology you think we might see later as having a big impact?

If you see something as having had a large negative impact, how can society counter it? What can your generation do to counter the negative or even turn lemons into lemonade over time?

LESSON 7.3. WHICH "YOUTH" ARE YOU?

Focus of Exploration

Differences between millennials, Gen Z, and Gen A.

Intro Questions / Thoughts for Student

We often divide people younger than boomers by age-groups:

- Gen Y (millennials)–1980 to 1995
- Gen Z—1996 to 2009
- Gen A—2010 to 2024 or so

Where do you fit? Why do you think we divide ages like that? What do people born those years have in common, especially in your group?

Why do you think the age-groups are divided at those points, at 1995–1996 and 2009–2010?

Activity

You will be surveying people from the three age-groups mentioned above. Try to interview at least three from each. You will ask them to rank the following activities they do while online from what they do least (1) to most (10). If there are some activities they do not do, include them in the rank by how much they think they would like to do those if they could.

- Listening to music
- Looking for general entertainment, like movies, to watch
- Watching a particular person's videos or following a particular person's broadcasts
- Reading for entertainment
- Gaming
- Texting/communicating with friends
- Using social apps to connect with friends and others
- Looking for things to do or places to eat
- Looking for advice
- Seeking education or learning about things

Once you have the rankings of at least three people from the three age-groups, add the numbers of each response in each age-group. For example, if your three millennials ranked "listen to music" as 1, 6, and 9, give it a total score of 16 (1 + 6 + 9). Then list the activities from lowest total score to highest. The activities with the highest totals are the ones that the age-group likes to do most.

Follow-Up Questions/Discussions

What are the similarities and differences between age-groups? Can you explain the differences?

If you see differences, you could say that is because each generation wants to do different things online because each generation values different things. On the other hand, the difference may be because of each group's age now. Gen A might be different now from Gen Z, but Gen A could be like Gen Z when Gen A gets to that age. When you have an outside factor that can affect your data or give another explanation for why things happen, it is called a *confounding variable*. Here, if we are trying to see if different generations have different values, the confounding variable is that the respondents are not the same age. Do you think you will change your online habits as you get older? How so?

Another factor is whether you interviewed enough people—or a wide enough variety of people—to get good data. Do you think the people you interviewed were a good representative sample? What do they have in common? What kinds of people might have been left out?

It's also important to interview respondents separately, not letting them hear or see each other's answers. Why do you think that is?

LESSON 7.4. JUST BETWEEN US

Focus of Exploration

Intimacy as a nudge.

Intro Questions / Thoughts for Students

The word "intimate" means something is close and personal. It's not for sharing with everyone but with just a very few, just one other, or only with yourself. Without telling, think of things you would consider to be intimate about yourself.

How do you feel when someone shares something intimate about themselves with you? Can it make you feel positively because you feel special or close to the person? Can it make you feel negatively because it's too personal and makes you feel uncomfortable?

How can you tell when someone is sharing something intimate or personal with you? What clues do you get, such as their telling you "It's private" or whispering?

Have you ever had someone tell you something you thought was intimate but then found out it really wasn't, like a "secret," but it turns out the person told many people? How did you feel?

Activity

Look for people online, especially people you or your friends follow, who seem to be trying to make their information intimate but still broadcast it to the general public. Look for things like the following:

- Words and phrases like "This is between you and me," "Only for my followers," "personal," or "exclusive"
- Cautioning that there are others who don't want you to know something
- Body movements like leaning in close to the camera or looking around as if to make sure no one else is listening
- Intimate settings like a small room or from their personal space
- Other mannerisms, like whispering (but you still can hear)

Follow-Up Questions/Discussions

Any posting, whether by text or video, will probably be seen by thousands, even if the poster says, "Don't tell." So why do they fake the intimacy? Does it make you more interested? Is that the point?

Even if you know the intimacy is faked, that the person who looks alone may be in a room with a cameraperson, a sound person, and even someone holding cue cards or a water bottle, you may still be drawn in. Why? Can it be also your setting? If you watch something alone in your personal space, does it feel more intimate?

What can you do when someone overshares or makes you feel uncomfortable by what they are sharing? Perhaps talk with your parents or other adults about if they have ever had that, and ask what is the best advice they have for you.

Telling people that there is an enemy, or someone who doesn't want you to know information, is a common tactic. If they are making it up or creating bad feelings against others just to get you to like them, is that OK? Can it lead to problems? What can you do to not be swayed by that?

Have you been asked to reveal something intimate online or IRL that you are not comfortable sharing? What can you do? It's good to have a plan so you are not caught in the moment. Perhaps speak with your parents or other adults about what you should do.

LESSON 7.5. WHAT I LIKE ABOUT VIEW

Focus of Exploration

Breaking down intuitive feelings into specifics.

Intro Questions / Thoughts for Students

What makes a video entertaining for you? Can you say (articulate) the things that attract you or make you like a video?

Activity

Watch videos you like. You can divide the videos between ones you really like or just sort of like. For each, make a checklist like the one below of everything that the video has:

Video: _____
Really like or sort of like? _____

- It features people just like me I can relate to.
- It has someone I admire or am a fan of.
- The video is funny.
- The video is suspenseful or tells a good story.
- The video makes me think about things, or I learn stuff from it.
- The video is fast-paced or full of action.
- I know the video is popular or liked by many.
- The video has good music.
- The video has good colors and visuals.
- Something else that jumped out at me was _____.

Follow-Up Questions/Discussions

Sometimes, when we are asked why we like something, it's hard to pin down. We may not even be aware exactly as to why. It's just our gut, also called our *intuition*. It can help to break things down so we can say "Yes, that's part of it" or "No, that's not it." Do you see any common traits about the videos you watched? Does the chart give you an idea of your overall likes?

Just because there is one trend, such as all the videos were funny, doesn't mean that's the only kind you like. Can you think of videos that don't meet the popular traits above that you like?

Can you do this with other things you like, even with things IRL? Try to break down why you like to go to certain places. Then look for other places that fit the common traits you can explore.

Can you do the same for things you don't like? Can you break down the factors or traits and narrow in on the ones that bother you the most? Once you do that, how will that help you in making choices later?

LESSON 7.6. DOUBLE TAKE

Focus of Exploration

Quantifying intuition.

Intro Questions / Thoughts for Students

When you judge something, do you first give it a gut grade, or do you give it a number rating? When do you go more with your first gut impression? When do you wait and slowly evaluate it?

Activity

First, make a list or scorecard of five things you like in videos. It can include the following:

- Popular
- Funny
- People like me
- Good music
- Good visuals
- Good story

Choose the five most important to you, including other categories. Now watch a couple of videos. They can be ones you like or don't like. It's better if the videos are generally similar to your categories (if you list "funny," don't watch a sad movie). Also, try to watch videos you have not seen before. Afterward you will grade them two ways, *in this order*:

- On a scale of one (worst) to ten (great!), what does your immediate gut give it? Don't think too long; just go with the first number that you feel fits.
- Now go through and rate the video one to ten in the same way for each of the five categories. Then total up the five category scores and divide that number by five to get its metric score.

Follow-Up Questions/Discussions

In comparing the gut score and the metric score for each video, how close were you? If they were close, is it because you have good intuition? We have to be a little careful of nudging ourselves with our own bias, making the category scores fit our gut. Do you ever do that in other cases, where you make your evaluation fit your first impression? How can you avoid that?

If your gut and metric scores did not match, was there any pattern as to which was always higher? Why do you think the scores were different? Which would you trust more? When is each a better assessor of your likes?

Teachers have been known to use this technique in grading papers. They give the paper an overall gut score based on their experience and expertise but also evaluate the paper by categories (called a rubric). Do you like the idea of your teacher grading that way? When would this be a good system for you to use to evaluate things, even choices you must make?

LESSON 7.7. KNOW OR NO!

Focus of Exploration

How much do parents and children know about each other's life?

Intro Questions / Thoughts for Students

For you and your parents, who knows more about each other's favorite media choices?

Activity

Each member of the family should fill in on a separate piece of paper the answers to the following statements:
- My favorite food is _____.
- My favorite celebrity is _____.
- My favorite music artist is _____.
- My favorite movie is _____.
- My favorite show to watch is _____.
- My favorite hobby, pastime, or thing to do in my free time is _____.
- The most misunderstood thing about me is that I am really _____.
- If I spent a whole day trying to make the world better, I would spend it by _____.
- If I could live like any kind of animal for a day, the animal would be a _____.
- The person whom I admire the most who is alive but not a family member is _____.
- In five years, I hope to be _____.

Read the questions. Everyone tries to correctly guess what the other people put as an answer. One point is awarded for each correct guess.

Follow-Up Questions/Discussions

Who knew other people in the family the best? Why do you think that is?

Have each member of the family prepare an entertainment night where the family has to listen to or watch that person's favorite music, movie, or show. The person can explain why he or she likes it. Why is it important to know, if not appreciate, what everyone likes?

Each person should get a weekend day where, for part of the day, everyone in the family helps out in the way that person said would make the world better. Then they should relax the way the person said he or she likes to spend as a pastime. Finish with the person's favorite food.

Can you come up with a plan where everyone gets a say or influence on what the family chooses? Some families use a choice wheel with every person's name so that each gets a turn. Would that work for your family?

LESSON 7.8. FUNNY THAT YOU THINK THAT'S FUNNY

Focus of Exploration

Understanding different generations by their humor.

Intro Questions / Thoughts for Students

Is *funny* the same for you as it was a couple of years ago? Why or why not?

How does what's funny change between different generations? How does funny change between genders—if at all? Are there things that are timelessly funny? Why?

Activity

For whatever is the age of the youngest participant, everyone in the family must find a video clip of what they thought was funny at that age. It can be a TV show or movie clip, a character, or a song.

Each will take a turn showing the clip to the others. They will explain why they thought it was funny (or still do). The other people will say what they think of it. Do they like it? Does it remind them of things they think are or thought were funny at that age?

Follow-Up Questions/Discussions

Do families have the same general idea of what is funny? If family members have different ideas of what is funny, is it because they are of different ages or grew up at different times? Do boys and girls generally have different ideas of funny? Where does the difference come from?

Some people say a lot can be learned about a person by what they think is funny. What does what each of you think is funny say about you and the rest of your family?

There is a theory of what is funny called the benign violation. The idea is that funny comes from something not going by our expectations or the rules of life, but no one gets hurt. If a person sits on a chair and it suddenly breaks, it can be funny, unless the person is physically hurt or has their feelings hurt. A pun breaks the rules of using words ("Orange you glad I didn't say banana!"). Can this theory explain all the video clips everyone had?

Do your friends agree about what is funny? Is there anything that just you think is funny? Why is that?

LESSON 7.9. NO TOLL TO THE TROLL

Focus of Exploration

Trolling.

Intro Questions / Thoughts for Students

Where is the line between saying you disagree with someone and being mean about it?

What is trolling? How does it differ from just countering what someone says?

Activity

Find a *discussion thread* or chat online or where there is a disagreement, even an argument. It can be a direct exchange or comments below a video or after an article. Read all the comments back and forth, but study the negative ones, the ones that don't just disagree with what has been said before but attack the poster with insults, accuse them of something, or make fun of them.

Follow-Up Questions/Discussions

The above technique is called an ad hominem attack. The comments attack the person they disagree with by calling them names, like stupid, or saying things about them ("I bet you never went to school" or "You are just one of those kinds of people"). It is considered a *fallacy* because it really doesn't address the issue. Imagine someone coming in and saying, "It's raining." The other person responds, "What do you know? Are you a weathercaster? You're ugly!"

Sometimes we don't see a put down to someone else as that bad because the thing being made fun of is not important to us ("You have many typos in your text, so you are stupid"). Is it more important how others see the put down or how the person on the receiving end sees it? What if someone made fun of you for something you cared about (like your hair), but others didn't as much? Would you want them to still stand up for you?

Sometimes the insults and trolling are kind of funny, even if they are insulting or off point. Should that sway you? We tend to like what makes us laugh, but how do we stay sided with a correct-but-not-funny opinion over a wrong-but-funny comment?

If you saw a friend troll someone, how would you respond? What factors might affect how you should respond? What if you didn't like the person being trolled? Should that matter?

What should you do if you are trolled? What is the best way to respond? If the troll is not so much interested in countering your point as in getting a reaction from you (that "feeds the troll"), what is the best response, if any? If the trolling is not reasonable or comes from someone who doesn't know you (or you don't really care what he or she thinks), should you be upset?

Studies show that people who disagree are meaner and troll more online than in person. Why do you think that is? Do you ever find you give different replies online than you do IRL?

LESSON 7.10. BUT WHAT ABOUT OTHER FALLACIES?

Focus of Exploration

Discussion diversions, whataboutism, and reductio ad absurdum.

Intro Questions / Thoughts for Students

Have you ever tried to have a discussion with someone but got frustrated because they tried to take the conversation to different topics or places? Maybe they brought up unrelated things you weren't talking about? How did you feel? What did you do?

Have you ever had someone rephrase what you were trying to say, but he or she turned it into something you were not saying, changing the meaning of what you meant? Maybe you told someone that you didn't like one shirt they had, and they responded, "So you hate the way I always dress!"

Activity

Look for a *discussion thread* or chat on a particular subject or point. It can be a direct exchange or comments below a video or after an article. Look if people go off topic or seem to take the conversation in a different direction than where it was going.

You might specifically look for two kinds of course-changing tactics:

- Whataboutism: Instead of addressing the thing being discussed, they bring up something off topic and try to relate it. They often start with "What about . . . ?"
- Reductio ad absurdum: This is a Latin phrase meaning someone takes an argument to crazy lengths to make it look bad. "If you start watching videos after school, you'll stop doing your homework altogether and will fail out of school!"

Look at how the post disrupts the thread and how the other posters respond. Do the responders try to get the conversation back on topic, or do they take the bait and go off course?

Follow-Up Questions/Discussions

When you found thread disruptions and things being taken off topic, did they seem more accidental or intentional? How can you tell? For the intentional ones, why do you think some people intentionally try to disrupt discussions? What is their goal? Is it *trolling*?

What were effective responses that you saw used against discussion thread disruptions? What did not work? There is always a choice between responding and trying to respond to the disruptor and just ignoring the attempted disruption. Which is more effective? Does it depend on the circumstance or disruption?

Some people call themselves disruptors and take pride in their disruptions. When is disruption OK, even something to be proud of? When it is not? Should a disruptor always have what they think is a better way in mind if they disrupt?

Do you think it is easier to disrupt discussions online or IRL? Why?

LESSON 7.11. ANCHORED EXPECTATIONS

Focus of Exploration

Anchoring, especially as to evaluating people. *Confirmation bias.*

Intro Questions / Thoughts for Students

When you think of positive descriptions of people, like smart or athletic, or negative adjectives, like clumsy or weird, do you think of specific people? Once you think of that person that way, do you think that affects how you see them and what they do after that? Do you ever change your view of them?

Have you ever been labeled a certain way or described based on how people first saw you? Did you ever get frustrated that people kept seeing you that way? What did you do?

Activity

Come up with a list of people you would generally put into positive categories, such as smart and athletic. List a reason why you think that they belong in that category, such as "Always gets the highest grade in math" or "Best soccer player." Without putting them down, can you then think of circumstances where that category doesn't apply to that person, such as "Smart in math but has trouble writing" or "Always organized but sometimes can't find their gym clothes"?

Now do this for people you associate with negative adjectives, like clumsy or not smart. Maybe think of people you think are socially awkward or boring. Can you find out where they do have strengths, even times they've acted counter to the negatives you have in mind?

Follow-Up Questions/Discussions

Once someone gets a reputation, they are often locked into that category. That is called *anchoring*. For example, if two people are thrown a ball and both drop it, for the one we think of as a bad athlete, we might think, "Typical!" But for the good athlete, we will think, "She's having a bad day." When is it OK to do that, and when is it not?

The reason you came up with circumstances where the people did not fit into a positive category was not to put them down but to realize no one fits into a positive category all the time. We all have positives, and at times, we don't meet our usual or expected positives. If you can't think of when a person doesn't fit into a positive all the time, maybe you don't know enough about their life.

Did you have trouble thinking of positives for the people you initially thought of as negative? Because of *confirmation bias*, we often ignore or don't remember any evidence that doesn't match how we prejudge things. Perhaps watch the people you associate with negative adjectives, but look for counter examples that you might have blocked out before. How can you better keep an open mind about people so that, even if they are sometimes in a category, you are better able to see when they don't fit that categorization or even should not be thought of that way?

The whole notion of putting people in general categories is appealing and can even be helpful at times. It can also be a trap leading to making bad judgments. How is this so?

Can we also be anchored in how we judge people by character, or at least what we think their character is: honest or dishonest, believable or unbelievable, nice or mean? Can that be a problem?

How do other people anchor their beliefs or categorizations of you? Do you like it? What can you do about it?

Glossary

ad hominem—When someone responds to an assertion not by addressing what was said but by attacking the person who said it. It is a main technique in *trolling*.
amygdala—The part of the brain that immediately processes memories and emotions, particularly fear and the fight-or-flight response. It begins its growth to adulthood with the onset of puberty and can be a dominant motivator in adolescent reactions until the maturation of the prefrontal cortex that regulates and balances emotional and rational reaction.
anchoring—When a chooser starts with an expectation or preconceived view and then evaluates the value or worth of things relative to that anchor, consciously or unconsciously.
aspirational motivation—When someone makes choices in hopes of being more like someone they admire or who is living in what they consider a better way. Youth often have aspirational motivation in imitating adult behavior. People also aspire to look and live like celebrities they admire or whom media highlights.
authentic, authenticity—A very important factor in youth choice in whether to believe or support a message or its messenger, especially in regards to influencers and other online personalities. Being authentic is to be outwardly true to one's actual nature rather than *posing* or trying to promote a product or opinion one doesn't really believe in (such as for money).
behavioral economics—An interdisciplinary study that combines psychology with traditional economics to study both the rational and nonrational factors in human choice.
benefit ratio—A quick method to weigh benefits to costs in making a choice. The subjective valuation of the benefits is divided by a similarly subjective valuation of the costs or risks. A ratio of one indicates benefits and costs

are equal. A ratio value below one indicates costs outweigh benefits, and a ratio value over one indicates benefits outweigh costs.

bling—Something owned that has value (*utility*) because other people know the person has it, and they admire or envy the person for having it. Bling is generally ostentatious to attract attention.

bots—A computer program that can respond to and interact with other programs or even humans. They do many positive functions, such as maintenance, but also can be used to masquerade as humans, such as liking a post by the thousands to give the false impression that many humans like that post.

buy-in point—The initial moment when a person interested in a topic or activity opts to spend time, money, and effort, as well as to risk other potential costs like public exposure to engage in that topic or activity.

choice architecture—The way a choice—say, as between option A and option B—is presented to a chooser. The architect designs or arranges the choice, often with a *nudge* to increase the likelihood of one option being chosen.

classification—According to Jean Piaget, a mental skill or tool used to sort and group things, such as for types of flowers, genres of games, or even "friends" and "enemies." It is acquired in early tween years and is heavily relied upon for understanding the world.

clickbait—Online content whose main purpose is to attract attention and encourage visitors to click on a link to a particular site to see more.

confirmation bias—When one collects data or analyzes information subconsciously to agree with one's already-held opinion. The investigator may only look for examples that agree with her view or ignore evidence that contradicts her opinion.

confounding variable—This is to be considered when comparing two things to see a relation, as a confounding variable is a third factor or thing that might affect the relationship. For example, there are more shark attacks at the same time people eat more ice cream. One does not cause the other, however. The confounding variable is the heat of summer that makes more people both eat ice cream and swim in the ocean.

conscious factors in decisions—Factors which we are aware of at the time they are influencing our choices. In contrast are *subconscious factors and decisions*.

conspicuous consumption—Spending money or consuming goods and services intentionally in public so that people will admire or be jealous of the consumer.

content creator—A person who writes or designs the substance in a video or on a website. This can be distinguished from the online presenter. Often, however, one person does those jobs.

context—Evaluating something by considering the greater circumstances, especially how the thing being evaluated compares to other things like it.

correlation—When two or more things have an association with each other, especially in terms of time. They can happen at the same time or, often, one right after the other. People often draw *inferences* about how things are related because of correlation, such as cause and effect. Such inferences may or may not be true.

cost-benefit analysis—A process by which people can make rational choices—say, between option A and option B—by comparing four factors: (1) the benefits of option A, (2) the benefits of option B, (3) the costs of option A, and (4) the costs of option B.

default choice, default choice architecture—Designing a choice so that, if the chooser makes no definitive choice or does not take action, the choice is made for them.

delayed gratification—Resisting a more immediate but lesser reward in order to obtain a greater reward later.

discussion thread—An online series of comments usually formed by an initial question or comment followed up by other people posting their opinions or reactions to the original post or subsequent ones.

drivers—Subconscious desires that tweens most often respond to in messaging.

echo chambers—Online, it is an environment or space, such as a *discussion thread*, where a person only encounters information or opinions that reflect and reinforce their own views. This can amplify the single point of view and its hold on people.

economics—Economics is the study of how people make choices in regard to scarce resources, such as having limited money, material, or time.

eye candy—Visual images that are superficially attractive and entertaining, though often intellectually undemanding, designed to grab a person's immediate attention.

fad—An intense but usually short-lived excitement for something or some activity, such as Hula-Hoops, Pet Rocks, internet crazes (like challenges), or a fashion style. The popularity is usually driven by FOMO, and young people are particularly susceptible to joining in.

fallacy—When one makes a point or bases a belief not on facts or reasoning but on bad logic, such as an ad hominem or whataboutism.

FOMO—An acronym for fear of missing out, it's a bad or uneasy feeling that one is not being included in a popular trend, which makes the person want to participate in the trend whether they like it or not.

gamification—Adding gamelike elements, such as challenges, competition, or rewards, to an activity to make it more appealing.

grabber—A dramatic opening in a video or other presentation that captures and draws in an audience, like a mystery or cliff-hanger. It's done to draw in the video consumer to commit more time to watching longer. It is sometimes done to lower the relative *transaction cost* by raising the potential reward of watching an ad that follows the grabber.

group pressure—Also called *crowding*, it is a nudge by surrounding people exerted on a person in making a choice. It can be direct or indirect, intentional or unintentional, and it arises from the sheer size, presence, and importance of the people to the chooser. If exerted by peers rather than the general public or family, it is peer pressure.

heuristics—Mental shortcuts or rules of thumb people create to more quickly and easily understand, categorize, and respond to a situation, especially on making choices.

inferences—Preliminary conclusions based on the information one has. After a person has gathered facts, one makes an inference based on the evidence as to what is the most likely or probable explanation for the facts. When you look outside and see it is wet and people have umbrellas up, you can make an inference it is raining. You don't have to be 100 percent sure (it could be a sprinkler getting people wet), but it is your best conclusion until you get more evidence.

internalized, internalizing—Assimilation of outside messaging into one's subconscious so that it becomes a part of one's beliefs or an internal influence on one's behavior.

IRL—Short for "In real life," it's a common shorthand used to designate the physical world versus online; for example, "IRL you don't get unlimited lives like you do in the game."

media literacy—An interdisciplinary study that combines behavioral economics and the study of media messaging, education, and other disciplines with the goal of educating and empowering message recipients to understand how media messaging affects choice making so that they can then make more independent, informed choices for themselves.

metadecision—As we use it, a metadecision is a general, nonspecific choice to generally choose something or, at least, to head in that direction. It should be a first step to a more focused, well-considered decision, but it often remains the extent of a choice. "I'll check my messages" is a metadecision, while "I will check my messages for thirty minutes but then get back to work" is the follow-through, refining choice that could be made secondarily, though we often don't.

mobbing—Online, this is the group bullying of a perceived "enemy" by one directing a wave of negative comments at a person, undermining that person's reputation by multiple negative comments, or causing disruption to that person's life through various online means.

new media—A designation often used to indicate more recent and interactive mass media, such as social apps or videos that allow more consumer interaction with the content creators. It is used to distinguish from *old media.*

newbie—An inexperienced newcomer to a game or experience. Not knowing the rules or tricks, newbies, also called *noobs*, often make mistakes or can be exploited by more experienced people.

nonrational choices—Choices made, at least in part, based on nonquantifiable factors or on factors beyond objective reason and facts. They can be *conscious* or *subconscious*. They are not to be confused with *irrational* choices, which imply a rejection of rational factors to make a bad choice.

nudge—In behavioral economics, this is a suggestion or emphasis to choose one option over another. It is not a command to choose one in particular, but it presents or puts one option in a superior position to favor the odds that it will be chosen. As we use it, nudges are supplied at the moment of choice.

old media—A designation used to indicate more generally broadcast, less-interactive mass media, such as movies and television. It is used to distinguish from *new media.*

persona—An image or personality a person presents publicly. It may be the same as their true, *authentic* self, or it may be very different, but it is generally the personality people think of in regard to that person.

plug—As opposed to an ad by a third party, a plug is when the person in the video or the content provider directly mentions or otherwise promotes something, such as an item to buy, another video, or even him- or herself.

pop—A hard-to-express—ineffable—description used in entertainment. It is when an ad, statement, or action makes people stop and focus on the content, usually with a wondrous "Whoa!" fascination that keeps them engaged. It's often a surprise or a "I can't believe they did that!" moment in entertainment, though it is often preplanned by the presenters.

posing—dressing or acting in an artificial way so as to try to give a false impression of who a person is. It is usually used in reference to an unsuccessful attempt to pass one's self off in a way that is not *authentic.*

prefrontal cortex—The part of the brain that oversees the executive function of regulating and balancing emotional and rational reaction to stimuli. It is not fully developed until about age twenty-five.

presumptive choice—This is when a choice is presented with the choice options implicitly limited or built in as predecided one way or another, even if the overall choice is presented as the decider's choice. Parents are good at this! A form is a *pretend choice,* also called a false choice, when a decision is presented as a choice, but the options are either so imbalanced in cost or effect that there is only one rational option, or the options amount to the same thing so there is no real choice.

quantifiable, quantifying—When the state of something can be measured or expressed as a number or is able to be compared to other quantifiable things. While things like amount or duration are more quantifiable, things like intensity of feeling are more difficult to quantify precisely.

reductio ad absurdum—A fallacy where someone takes another person's position and blows it out of proportion, such as its consequences. "If you don't agree with me now, you never were my friend, and you'll probably stab me in the back every time I say something!"

resources—In economics, resources are things used to make other things. More formally called *factors in production*, they are divided into *land* (physical material and resources), *labor* (the workforce to make it), *capital* (tools and machines for making things), and *entrepreneurship* (know-how, determination, and other brainpower).

sample size and **sampling error**—A sample size is the part one uses to assess the greater whole. It can be an object, such as one apple to judge a bushel, a group of people to make judgments about the group they represent, or a time period to make an estimate how the rest of the time is used. A sampling error occurs when one makes false judgments or conclusions based on a sample that does not accurately represent the greater whole.

scarce, scarcity—When there is not enough of a resource to meet demand for it. In contrast is something being *rare*, which means it is few in number regardless of demand for it.

self-fulfilling prophecy—Often arising because of *confirmation bias,* it is when we make a situation turn out the way we expected it would. We often do this subconsciously, such as our expecting not to win in a game makes us not play as well or even give up.

self-swaying—When a chooser predisposes him- or herself into a choice preference before the moment of choice by approaching the moment with a fixed rule of thumb or *heuristic.*

seriation—according to Jean Piaget, this is a mental skill or tool used to arrange things within a group by a consistent value or measure, such as by size or price. Like *classification*, it is acquired in early tween years and is relied upon for understanding the world.

slacktivism—Supporting political or social causes through online activities and social apps, such as discussing the issue, creating petitions, and fundraising. The name was coined to imply that such virtual support is not as effortful or impactful as activism in real life.

social calculus—This is the act of having to be simultaneously mentally engaged and apart from a social interaction to assess what is going on. The person then must calculate what is an appropriate response. It might be assessing whether a comment was meant honestly or sarcastically and how one should react to it. It can be tiring because one has to both participate in and assess what is going on at the same time, causing tension and discomfort.

social science—Social sciences are devoted to the study of human behavior, including how and why humans do what we do. Social sciences include psychology, sociology, and economics. Different from social sciences are the physical sciences, like chemistry, astronomy, and physics.

stakeholder—Someone who has an interest by getting more or less, depending on the choice made. They often are not the actual chooser, but they are affected by the choice.

stereotype—A broad or fixed idea of a person or thing that we assume is true for every other person or thing like it. It ignores individual differences and (often incorrectly) assumes that if we think A and B are alike in one way, they must be alike in other specific ways.

subconscious factors and decisions—Those factors or choices which we are unaware of at the time they are in our thoughts or consideration, though they still have an impact on our making a choice. In contrast are *conscious factors in decisions*.

sways—Historical events and messaging in one's past that create, with other events, *internalized* preferences in people. Sways cause choosers to arrive at a decision moment already preferring one choice over another, even before *nudges* act at the moment of choosing.

transaction cost—The time, physical and mental effort, money, and other resources needed to choose an option. Basically, it is what it will take for a person to do or obtain something.

trolling—Deliberately seeking to upset or antagonize a person. It is often done online by posting inflammatory, nonsensical, outrageous, or otherwise offensive comments. Trolling is one form of cyberbullying.

tween—Roughly the period of life from ten to twelve years of age. It is when hormonal changes and abstract thought begin to affect physical and mental development. In American education, it is usually the time of middle school.

utility—In economics, it is the satisfaction or "goodness" one gets from consuming or using something.

whataboutism—a fallacy where someone tries to get people off one topic by comparing it to another. "You think this is unfair? What about the unfairness of people living in poverty?" A subset is a *tu quoque* (you also), where the responder deflects criticism by suggesting the speaker does the same thing. "I'm selfish for taking all the pizza! What about last week, when you made me wait while you had to finish getting ready?" This is sometimes intentionally used to disrupt a *discussion thread*.

Bibliography

Ansorge, Rick. "Piaget Stages of Development." WebMD. Last updated March 12, 2023. https://www.webmd.com/children/piaget-stages-of-development.
Arthur, Charles. "How Laptops Took over the World." *The Guardian*, October 28, 2009. https://www.theguardian.com/technology/2009/oct/28/laptops-sales-desktop-computers#:~:text=In%20the%20US%2C%20laptops%20first.
Becker, Maren, Nico Wiegand, and Werner J. Reinartz. "Does It Pay to Be Real? Understanding Authenticity in TV Advertising." *Journal of Marketing* 83, no. 1 (December 4, 2018): 24–50. https://doi.org/10.1177/0022242918815880.
Brafman, Ori, and Rom Brafman. *Sway: The Irresistible Pull of Irrational Behavior*. New York: Doubleday, 2009.
Canales, Katie. "Silicon Valley Says Kids over the Age of 13 Can Handle the Big, Bad World of Social Media. Experts Say That's the Result of a 'Problematic' 1990s Internet Law." *Business Insider*, January 14, 2022. https://www.businessinsider.com/why-you-must-be-13-facebook-instagram-problematic-law-coppa-2022-1#:~:text=Kids%20will%20be %20exposed%20to%20the%20internet%2C%20regardless%20of%20rules&text=Facebook%20and%20most%20other%20platforms.
Carey, Benedict. "Making Sense of the 'Mob' Mentality." *New York Times*, January 12, 2021, Science. https://www.nytimes.com/2021/01/12/science/crowds-mob-psychology.html.
Clear, James. "The Marshmallow Experiment and the Power of Delayed Gratification." Published January 23, 2014. https://jamesclear.com/delayed-gratification.
Cloudfare. "What Is Swatting? How to Prevent Swatting." Accessed July 15, 2022. https://www.cloudflare.com/learning/security/glossary/what-is-swatting/.
DeadricBaguette. "Why was Pewdiepie so easily forgiven for saying the n word?" Reddit, February 5, 2022. https://www.reddit.com/r/ask/comments/slb4lw/why_was _pewdiepie_ so_easily_forgiven_for_saying/?sort=new.

Federal Trade Commission. "Children's Online Privacy Protection Rule ('COPPA')." Published July 25, 2013. https://www.ftc.gov/legal-library/browse/rules/childrens-online-privacy-protection-rule-coppa.

Friel, Sonya. "Modern-Day Youth Activism: Youth Engagement in the Digital Age." *Global Fund for Children*, September 9, 2021. https://globalfundforchildren.org/story/modern-day-youth-activism-youth-engagement-in-the-digital-age/.

Frost, Robert. "The Road Not Taken." Poetry Foundation. Accessed. https://www.poetryfoundation.org/poems/44272/the-road-not-taken.

Gojak, Linda. "Algebra: Not 'If' but 'When'—National Council of Teachers of Mathematics." National Council of Teachers of Mathematics (NCTM). Published December 3, 2013. https://www.nctm.org/News-and-Calendar/Messages-from-the-President/Archive/Linda-M_-Gojak/Algebra_-Not-_If_-but-_When_/.

Goleman, Daniel. *Emotional Intelligence: Why It Can Matter More than IQ.* New York: Bantam Books, 1995.

Hammond, A. M. "What Does the Internet Teach Your Teen about Sex?" *Psychology Today*, September 16, 2019. https://www.psychologytoday.com/us/blog/brainstorm/201909/what-does-the-internet-teach-your-teen-about-sex.

Henderson, David. "Richard H. Thaler." Econlib. Accessed December 26, 2022. https://www.econlib.org/library/Enc/bios/Thaler.html.

Howson, Nichole. "Why Being Authentic on Social Media Is Important." AIM Social. Published October 27, 2018. https://aimsmmarketing.com/why-being-authentic-on-social-media-is-important/#:~:text=Being%20Authentic%20helps%20create%20a.

Licano, Leslie. "Council Post: Keeping It Real: The Importance of Having an Authentic Social Media Presence." *Forbes*, September 13, 2019. https://www.forbes.com/sites /forbesagencycouncil/2019/09/13/keeping-it-real-the-importance-of-having-an-authentic-social-media-presence/?sh=44353f37110f.

Luxton, David D., Jennifer D. June, and Jonathan M. Fairall. "Social Media and Suicide: A Public Health Perspective." *American Journal of Public Health* 102, no. S2 (May 2012): S195–200. https://doi.org/10.2105/ajph.2011.300608.

Manjusha, J., S. Mitra, and L. Bhooshetty. "Is Nostalgia Marketing a Game-Changer for Toy Industry?" *Ilkogretim Online* 20, no. 5 (2021): 1820–31. https://doi.org/10.17051/ilkonline.2021.05.200.

McNally, Catherine. "Nearly 1 in 4 Households Don't Have Internet—and a Quarter Million Still Use Dial-Up." Reviews.org. Published August 17, 2021. https://www.reviews.org /internet-service/how-many-us-households-are-without-internet-connection/.

McNeal, James U. *Kids as Customers: A Handbook of Marketing to Children.* New York: Lexington Books, 1992.

Otterbring, Tobias, and Michał Folwarczny. "Firstborns Buy Better for the Greater Good: Birth Order Differences in Green Consumption Values." *Personality and Individual Differences* 186 (February 2022): 111353. https://doi.org/10.1016/j.paid.2021.111353.

Pew Research Center. "Mobile Fact Sheet." Published April 7, 2021. https://www.pewresearch.org/internet/fact-sheet/mobile/.

———. "Political Polarization in the American Public." Published June 12, 2014. https://www.pewresearch.org/politics/2014/06/12/political-polarization-in-the-american-public/.

PurposeFocusCommitment. "The Rice and the Chess Board Story—the Power of Exponential Growth." Medium. Published April 9, 2020. https://purposefocuscommitment.medium.com/the-rice-and-the-chess-board-story-the-power-of-exponential-growth-b1f7bd70aaca.

Repko, Allen F., Rick Szostak, and Michelle Phillips Buchberger. *Introduction to Interdisciplinary Studies.* Los Angeles: Sage, 2017.

Rozhon, Tracie. "A Lingerie Maker Returns to Its Racier Past." *New York Times*, October 25, 2002. https://www.nytimes.com/2002/10/25/business/a-lingerie-maker-returns-to-its-racier-past.html.

Rutter, Claire. "PewDiePie Begs for Forgiveness for Victims of Offensive Prank." *Mirror*, January 17, 2017. https://www.mirror.co.uk/3am/celebrity-news/pewdiepie-begs-forgiveness-victims-offensive-9635474.

Siegel, David L., Timothy J. Coffey, and Gregory Livingston. *The Great Tween Buying Machine: Marketing to Today's Tweens.* Ithaca, NY: Paramount Marketing, 2001.

Statista. "Internet Penetration United States 2017." Published 2017. https://www.statista.com/statistics/209117/us-internet-penetration/.

Tarawneh, Rawan. "How Does the Internet Affect Brain Function?" The Ohio State University Wexner Medical Center. Published February 26, 2020. https://wexnermedical.osu.edu /blog/how-internet-affects-your-brain#:~:text=Recent%20research%20suggests %20that%20excess.

"The Truth behind 6 Disturbing Cyberbullying Cases That Turned into Suicide Stories." Washington Township Public Schools. Accessed July 15, 2022. https://www.wtps.org /cms/lib8/NJ01912980/Centricity/Domain/745/The%20truth%20behind%206%20disturbing%20cyberbullying%20cases%20that%20turned%20into%20suicide.pdf.

Vice Media. "The Culture of Content Consumption." Published August 2019. https://ontariocreates.ca/uploads/Business_Intelligence/en/GENZ_The_Culture_of_Content_Consumption.pdf.

Wallace, Elaine, Pedro Torres, Mário Augusto, and Maryana Stefuryn. "Do Brand Relationships on Social Media Motivate Young Consumers' Value Co-Creation and Willingness to Pay? The Role of Brand Love." *Journal of Product & Brand Management* 31, no. 2 (June 15, 2021): 189–205. https://doi.org/10.1108/jpbm-06-2020-2937.

Wallenbrock, Emma. "Hordes of Teens in Suits Are Showing Up to the Minions Movie. The Studio, for Once, Did the Right Thing." *Slate*, July 7, 2022. https://slate.com/culture/2022/07/minion-rise-of-gru-box-office-gentleminions-meme.html.

Wasserman, Jim. *High Schoolers, Meet Media Literacy.* Lanham, MD: Rowman & Littlefield, 2019.

———. "Saving the Day." *HumbleDollar*, February 12, 2022. https://humbledollar.com/2022/02/saving-the-day/.

Wasserman, Jim, and David W. Loveland. *Middle Schoolers, Meet Media Literacy*. Lanham, MD: Rowman & Littlefield, 2019.

WegENT. "Survey: Do NFL Fans Stay Loyal to Their Teams after Moving?" *Wegryn Enterprises* (blog). October 12, 2021. https://wegrynenterprises.com/2021/10/12/survey-do-nfl-fans-stay-loyal-to-their-teams-after-moving/.

West, Patricia M., Christina L. Brown, and Stephen J. Hoch. "Consumption Vocabulary and Preference Formation." *Journal of Consumer Research* 23, no. 2 (September 1996): 120. https://doi.org/10.1086/209471.

About the Authors

Jim Wasserman is a former business litigation attorney and, for over twenty years, a media literacy, economics, and humanities teacher. He has written extensively on education generally and media literacy specifically, including a three-book series on how to introduce media literacy to elementary, middle, and high school students.

Jiab Wasserman is a former industrial engineer and bank executive who became a vice president at Bank of America. Since retiring, she has become a trailblazer in advocating for gender, ethnic, and immigrant equity in the workplace and in education. She has written about the financial world and financial practices for several years and continues to be a regular contributor on the subject.

www.ingramcontent.com/pod-product-compliance
Lightning Source LLC
Chambersburg PA
CBHW020852160426
43192CB00007B/891